Understanding
Creation

Understanding
Creation

With best wishes for my neighbor and friend Byron,

Humberto

July 2012

**Answers
to questions
on faith and
science**

L. JAMES GIBSON *and* HUMBERTO M. RASI, co-editors

Pacific Press® Publishing Association
Nampa, Idaho
Oshawa, Ontario, Canada
www.pacificpress.com

Cover design by Gerald Lee Monks
Cover design resources from iStockPhoto.com
Inside design by Michelle C. Petz

Copyright © 2011 by Pacific Press® Publishing Association
Printed in the United States of America
All right reserved

The authors assume full responsibility for the accuracy of all facts and quotations as cited in this book.

You can obtain additional copies of this book by calling toll-free 1-800-765-6955 or by visiting www.adventistbookcenter.com.

ISBN 13: 978-0-8163-2428-6
ISBN 10: 0-8163-2428-X

11 12 13 14 15 • 5 4 3 2 1

Contents

Introduction

God created humans to be naturally inquisitive beings. From our earliest years we ask questions and keep doing so throughout life. We first want to understand our place within our circle of relationships. Our observation of and experience with nature—flowers, birds, animals, trees, rivers, stars—further stimulates our curiosity. As we grow up, we want to know how things work, to understand our place in the world, and to discover our purpose in life. During the course of our studies, our field of inquiry continues to expand exponentially.

Many of our initial questions become deeper and more complex. Where did humans come from? How did life originate? What factors led to the appearance of the earth, the sun, the planets, and the entire universe? Why do many of the laws we perceive in nature seem both so reliable and yet so mysterious? Is there a Being or Force behind the intricate structure of nature as we know it—from the components of the tiniest cell to the vast galaxies of our expanding cosmos? Religion, philosophy, science, literature, and the arts respond in diverse ways to these intriguing questions.

For centuries Western culture operated within the context of a

Christian worldview. For this reason, answers to those questions were anchored in the belief that God exists and is the Creator and Sustainer of everything in the universe. The Bible was generally considered a trustworthy revelation of God and the foundation of human belief, behavior, and hope. Many of the founders of modern science— Copernicus, Galileo, Kepler, Pascal, Boyle, Newton, Halley, and others— were believers of those central concepts, succinctly expressed by the apostle Paul in the first century of our era:

> For since the creation of the world God's invisible qualities—his eternal power and divine nature—have been clearly seen, being understood from what has been made, so that men are without excuse (Romans 1:20, NIV).

During the past two hundred years our culture, and particularly its scientific community, has been steadily moving away from the biblical-Christian worldview, and assuming a naturalistic stance that discounts any supernatural intervention in the origin, functioning, and maintenance of our world. As a result, two opposing philosophical views contend for allegiance in our time. They are outlined starkly by contemporary evolutionary biologist Douglas J. Futuyama in *Science on Trial* (Pantheon Books, 1983; p. 197):

> Creation and evolution, between them, exhaust the possible explanations for the origin of living things. Organisms either appeared on the earth fully developed or they did not. If they did not, they must have developed from pre-existing species by some process of modification. If they did appear in a fully developed state, they must indeed have been created by some omnipotent intelligence.

This book articulates twenty common questions about basic faith and science issues that Christians encounter in the course of their formal education, as they pursue advanced degrees, conduct research in various fields, and in their professional interactions. These topics are also frequently discussed in classrooms, addressed in the popular media, and debated in scientific conferences around the world.

The co-editors, in addition to contributing two of the chapters, have assembled an international group of experienced, Bible-believing scientists, researchers, and thinkers who have provided thoughtful answers to these foundational questions. Their respective fields of expertise include archaeology, astronomy, biology, chemistry, geology, history, paleontology, philosophy, and physics, as well as a number of subspecialties. Each author, naturally, assumes responsibility for the content of the chapter that bears his or her name.

All contributors share several convictions—that the biblical record contained in the book of Genesis is an essential component of Christian doctrine, that Christian faith and empirical science can work fruitfully together, that there is a basic difference between data and interpretation, and that our comprehension of truth is progressive. They believe that the more we learn about life and the universe, the stronger the case becomes for the existence of an infinitely wise and powerful Designer, who cares deeply about each human being and our entire planet. They are persuaded, on the basis of the Scriptures, that at the beginning God created a perfect habitat and harmonious life on this earth, but that as a result of the rebellion of the first pair of humans the entire creation has suffered the consequences. When these facts are disregarded, our understanding of nature and our practice of science becomes limited or misguided.

This book is addressed to readers who are curious about the questions that many ask as they observe and experience the natural world, and who are willing to consider a perspective that is different than the one currently in ascendance. The authors and editors have attempted to provide clear and honest answers, based on the best data available, in terms that will reach a broad circle of readers.

We wish to express our deep appreciation to each of the contributors to this volume for willingly sharing their expertise, preparing their contributions while actively involved in research, teaching, and administration. Of course, many more questions could have been posed, but these will serve as samples of an approach to subjects in faith and science from a coherent and integrated biblical worldview perspective. We thank Sylvia Rasi Gregorutti, who helped edit this volume, raising relevant issues, sharpening our focus, and smoothing the style. Our gratitude also goes to Jerry D. Thomas, vice president for product development at Pacific Press®, who supported this project from its inception and encouraged us along the way.

As you explore the issues, questions, and answers contained in this book, we wish to leave you with the profound wisdom of this ancient prayer:

From cowardice that shrinks from new truth,
From laziness that is content with half-truths,
From the arrogance that thinks it knows all truth—
O God of truth, deliver us!

L. James Gibson and Humberto M. Rasi
Loma Linda, California

Chapter 1

Why Do Different Scientists Interpret Reality Differently?

It is generally assumed that well-educated people who dedicate their professional lives to the scientific study of nature are able to approach their subjects with a dispassionate attitude. Using sophisticated equipment, they make careful observations, conduct experiments, develop hypotheses, propose theories, and arrive at objective conclusions in their respective areas of expertise.

Nevertheless, scientists applying the scientific method while using similar equipment to study the same aspect of nature can and do arrive at different conclusions. Why does this occur? The answer to this question can be found at three levels.

Differences in interpretation

Some of the common reasons for which scientists reach different conclusions in their research include factors such as the size and reliability of the sample data gathered, the adequacy of design in the experiments conducted, the precision of the equipment used, or simply human error. These factors can usually be remedied as other scientists learn of the results, review the procedures, data, and findings, then attempt to replicate the observations or experiments, and finally determine which of the conclusions or discoveries is favored by the weight of the evidence. This process is what makes science one of the most exciting human activities.

In March 1989, two established electrochemists—Martin Fleischmann and Stanley Pons—announced they had produced nuclear fusion at room temperature using heavy water and a palladium electrode. The reaction of the international scientific community was immediate, because the financial implications of producing energy at a very low cost are enormous. During the following years, similar experiments were conducted in many countries, conferences on the topic were convened, and well-funded research centers were established. However, most scientists have been unable to reproduce the original results and, as a result, have reached the conclusion that the evidence does not support the original claim.[1]

Different paradigms

A deeper reason for disagreement among scientists on a particular issue may be differing scientific paradigms, a concept proposed by Thomas S. Kuhn.[2] In his view, science is not an empirically autonomous and objective endeavor, but a collective activity influenced by social and historical factors. During periods of "normal science," he argued, the scientific community operates on a generally accepted model or paradigm. However, results that don't fit within those understandings gradually build up until a "paradigm shift" occurs. At that point, a new consensus and paradigm provide a new set of assumptions that serve as the basis for doing science. Kuhn provides the example of the paradigm shift that occurred when the Ptolemaic geocentric view of the universe was replaced by Copernicus' heliocentric model of the solar system.

Another significant paradigm shift occurred in the earth sciences in the 1960s, when the weight of evidence confirmed ideas that Alfred Wegener (1880–1930) had advanced regarding the movement of the continents. Up to his time, it was thought that the various continents were immovable and had been connected by land bridges that had later submerged. But during a conference in 1912, Wegener proposed that the continents had first been part of a supercontinent (which he named Pangaea) and that later they drifted apart. In 1915, he published this theory in a book on the origin of continents and oceans. For a few decades, his proposed theory of continental drift was rejected by the preeminent geologists, due in part to intellectual inertia and, more importantly, to the lack of concrete evidence and an explanatory mechanism. But after substantial new data accumulated, Wegener's idea that the continents have moved was accepted as valid and is now the working paradigm in geology, geophysics, oceanography, and paleontology.

The current debate surrounding climate change provides a prime example of a paradigm-based disagreement. For a number of years, a group of scientists have been analyzing data that suggest a recent steady increase in our planet's temperatures. Computer model projections indicate that if global warming continues at the current rate, humanity will face a series of irreversible catastrophes. However, scientists disagree over the cause; hence the two contrasting paradigms at play. One group believes that the recent rise in temperatures is caused by natural climate cycles, which occur independent of human activity. Scientists using this paradigm emphasize the correlation between solar cycles and global temperatures. The other group believes that human activity is responsible for the increase in global temperatures. Scientists using this paradigm look for correlations between carbon and other emissions and indices of climate change. Of course, the ethical, economic, and political implications of this debate and its outcome complicate the issue. However, once this controversy is settled, a paradigm shift may have occurred, followed by more government policies or international mandates regarding effluents and pollution.[3]

At a more profound level, however, disagreements among scientists in several fields may be based on what rules should be applied in interpreting the origin of the natural world and its operating laws. Is there or is there not a Supreme Being who designed, created, and sustains the universe and its creatures?[4] This debate has been growing in intensity since the 1800s, particularly after Charles Darwin published in 1859 his book *On the Origin of Species*. Why do honest scientists disagree on this fundamental question? And, more importantly, is this an issue that can be settled by applying the scientific method? These questions lead us to consider the concept of worldviews.[5]

Worldviews and their implications

All humans, including scientists, develop a worldview through which they understand, interpret, and explain reality at its most fundamental level. Since we all wish to make sense of our experiences, our personal worldview serves as a mental map that orients us in our decisions and actions.[6] No philosophy degree is needed to possess a worldview. Even scientists are unable to approach the study of a particular object, organism, or phenomenon with a completely objective attitude—all bring to their investigation a particular set of understandings and assumptions regarding the universe and life—a worldview.[7]

Our individual worldview begins to take shape during adolescence and matures in young adulthood. It is initially the result of various influences—family, studies, media, and the surrounding culture. We continue to adjust its contours throughout our life due to new information and experiences.

At its most basic, a worldview answers four questions:[8]

Who am I?—The origin, nature, and purpose of human beings.
Where am I?—The nature and extent of reality.
What is wrong?—The cause of injustice, suffering, evil, and death.
What is the solution?—Ways of overcoming these obstacles to human fulfillment.

Of course, this set of basic questions could easily be expanded.[9] Ultimately, our worldview provides the foundation for our values and is reflected in our decisions and behavior. It influences, for example, our choice of vocation or profession, our relationship with other humans, the way we spend our financial resources, our use of technology, our attitude toward the environment, and even our socio-political decisions regarding issues of justice and peace.

The answers we give to the questions listed above can be linked by an overarching story (a meta-narrative) that integrates concepts of origin, purpose, meaning, and destiny. Imagine, for example, how two well-trained scientists with different worldviews—for example, a Bible-believing

Christian and a neo-Darwinian evolutionist—would structure and articulate their overarching narrative from their individual perspectives.

It is worthwhile to note that the impact of the scientist's worldview on research questions, methods, and results has been much more significant in the historical and cosmic sciences than in the experimental and mathematical sciences.

Major worldviews

Through recorded history, humans have adopted three major worldviews, which can be summarized as follows:

Theism posits the existence of a personal God who is Creator and Sovereign of the universe. This Supreme Being is separate from His creation but acts in its operation.

Pantheism identifies an impersonal deity with the forces and workings of nature. Reality consists of the universe plus god. They are mutually interpenetrating and interacting.

Naturalism assumes that reality consists of the material universe operating according to natural laws plus nothing else.

Although there are varieties and subsets of the three major worldviews, these can be outlined in the following manner:

It is well-known that modern science emerged during the 1500s and 1600s within the context of a theistic culture that was predominantly Christian. Pioneer thinkers and scientists in various disciplines such as Copernicus, Galileo, Kepler, Pascal, Boyle, Newton, Halley, and others believed in a creator God who had established operating laws in the universe and nature that could be discovered and applied for the benefit of humanity. In contrast, cultures in which pantheism predominated did not offer a favorable milieu for scientific endeavors because nature was seen as divine and therefore sacred.[10]

Some more recent approaches seek to establish connections among these basic worldviews. Theistic evolution, for example, attempts to bridge Christianity and naturalism, proposing that God operates in the world through the process of evolution. Neo-pantheism, on its part, suggests close links between scientific materialism and religious mysticism.[11]

Contrasting worldviews

During the last 150 years, the scientific community has gradually moved away from its Christian roots and has assumed a naturalistic worldview that discounts any supernatural intervention or transcendent meaning. It is within this worldview that the sciences are generally taught, research is conducted, and articles are rejected or accepted for publication. The most popular current expression of this worldview is secular humanism.[12] The contrast between the basic tenets of biblical Christianity and secular humanism—as representatives of theism and naturalism—can be summarized as follows:

Key concept	Biblical Christianity	Secular Humanism
Prime reality	A transcendent God who acts in the universe and can be known by human beings on the basis of His self-revelation.	Inanimate matter and energy.
Origin of the universe and life	Both were created by God by the power of His word to operate on the basis of cause-and-effect laws in a system He sustains and in which He freely acts.	The universe is eternal or began with a sudden cosmic explosion and operates on the basis of cause-and-effect laws in a closed system. Life appeared from nonlife by chance and natural laws.
Means of knowing truth	God's self-disclosure perceived through His created works, in the Scriptures, and especially in the person of Jesus Christ. God also communicates with humans through their conscience and reason illumined and guided by the Holy Spirit.	Through human reason and intuition, working through and confirmed by the scientific method. For others, truth is beyond human reach, if it exists at all. Ultimately, all knowledge and truth are relative to culture, time, and place.

Key concept	Biblical Christianity	Secular Humanism
Origin and nature of human beings	Physical-spiritual beings created perfect in God's image, capable of free moral decisions, now in an imperfect condition.	Humans are merely another form of living organism that originated through unguided evolutionary processes.
Human history	Ultimately, a meaningful sequence of events, guided by free human decisions, but supervised by God, who acts in fulfillment of His overall plan for the good of His creatures.	Unpredictable and without overarching purpose; guided both by human decisions and by natural forces beyond human understanding and control.
Basis of morality	The unchanging character of God (merciful and just), revealed in the life of Jesus Christ and in the Scriptures.	The majority opinion, contemporary customs, cultural traditions, particular circumstances, or a combination thereof.

Key concept	Biblical Christianity	Secular Humanism
Cause of the human predicament	Conscious rebellion against God and His principles; an attempt to enthrone humans as autonomous creatures; as a result, the image of God in humans has been defaced and the entire world suffers.	Ignorance of true human potential, bad laws, incompetent government, lack of human cooperation, a natural human flaw, among others.
Solution to the human predicament	A spiritual rebirth: trust in divine forgiveness through Jesus Christ, which leads to a life of loving obedience to God, proper self-understanding, inner peace, and harmonious relationships.	Improved education, more support for science, technological progress, just laws, competent government, improved human tolerance and cooperation, eugenics, stronger care of the biosphere, among others.
Death	An unconscious parenthesis until the day of God's final judgment. (Other Christians: entrance into another conscious state.)	The final end of human existence in all its dimensions.

Key concept	Biblical Christianity	Secular Humanism
Ultimate human destiny	Transformed beings living eternally in a new earth or eternal annihilation. (Other Christians: eternal punishment.)	Nothingness and oblivion.

The biblical worldview narrative

The existence of God and whether He created the universe and life are, by definition, questions beyond the scope and the capability of naturalistic science. The answers to such questions rely on worldview assumptions, which are based on evidence that may or may not be satisfactory to equally competent scientists. Yet, these answers influence the development of hypotheses and theses and the interpretation of data in many scientific endeavors.

From the beginning of modern science, Christian scientists have worked based on the premise that the Creator of the universe and life is the same God that communicated with humans through the Scriptures. Christians who anchor their convictions in the Bible develop a worldview and narrative that, as interpreted by Seventh-day Adventists, include seven key moments in cosmic history:

Creation in heaven. At some time in the remote past, God creates a perfect universe and populates it with intelligent and free creatures.

Rebellion in heaven. An exalted creature rebels against God's principles and, after a struggle, is banished to earth with his followers.

Creation on earth. During six days in the recent past, God makes this planet inhabitable and creates plant and animal life, including the first pair of humans, who are endowed with free will.

Fall on earth. Tempted by the rebel creature, the first couple disobeys God and the entire web of life on this planet suffers the consequences, including a devastating global flood.

Redemption. Jesus Christ, the Creator Himself, comes to earth to rescue fallen humans, offering them free salvation and power to live a transformed life.

Second coming. At the end of time, Christ returns in glory as promised, and grants immortality to those who have accepted His offer of forgiveness and salvation.

Consummation. After a millennium passes, Christ returns to execute final judgment, eliminates evil, and restores the entire creation to its original perfection, which will last forever.

The biblical worldview and its overarching narrative are attractive because they provide an internally coherent answer to key worldview questions. This worldview offers a satisfactory explanation for what we learn, discover, or experience in real life, and gives meaning and transcendent hope to human's deepest desires. At the same time, our Christian worldview is always in development, under the guidance of the Holy Spirit, because our understanding of God's revelation is limited and progressive.[13]

Conclusion

As we have seen, equally capable scientists arrive at different conclusions due to methodological factors, to working within different paradigms, or to the contrasting worldviews they have embraced. Nevertheless, Christian scientists who conduct research from the biblical worldview perspective can comfortably work alongside other scientists who may not share their assumptions and yet jointly achieve meaningful findings and respectable conclusions. Those who accept the biblical narrative as true and reliable enjoy the advantage of having at their disposal additional options and insights provided by the Creator in the Scriptures, which can generate research questions that may lead to fruitful hypotheses, explanations, and discoveries.[14]

Humberto M. Rasi received his college education in his homeland, Argentina, completed a PhD in Hispanic literature and history at Stanford University, and a postdoctoral fellowship at Johns Hopkins University. He served as professor and dean of graduate studies at Andrews University, as editorial vice president at Pacific Press®, and world director of the Education Department for the Seventh-day Adventist Church. He co-founded the Institute for Christian Teaching, launched the journal College and University Dialogue, *and has published many articles and edited several books. Although retired, he continues to lecture, publish, and coordinate projects in international higher education.*

References

[1] See, for example, Fred Nadis, *Undead Science: Science Studies and the Afterlife of Cold Fusion* (New Brunswick, NJ: Rutgers University Press, 2002) or Hideo Kozima, *The Science of the Cold Fusion Phenomenon* (Oxford: Elsevier Ltd., 2006).

[2] See Thomas S. Kuhn, *The Structure of Scientific Revolutions* (Chicago: University of Chicago Press, 1962, 1970, 1996).

[3] Clusters of scientific fields tend to operate within a shared paradigm, which Thomas Kuhn called a "disciplinary matrix" in the postscript to the 1970 edition of his book. Consider the assumptions, methods, and preferred research questions that are common, for example, to the historical sciences (archaeology, geology, paleontology), or to the cosmic sciences (astronomy, astrophysics, space science), or to the experimental sciences (biology, chemistry, physics), or the behavioral sciences (psychology, psychiatry, sociology).

[4] See Roy A. Clouser, *The Myth of Religious Neutrality: An Essay on the Hidden Role of Religious Belief in Theories,* rev. ed. (Notre Dame, Indiana: University of Notre Dame Press, 2005).

[5] See David K. Naugle, *Worldview: The History of a Concept* (Grand Rapids, MI: William B. Eerdmans Publ. Co., 2002).

[6] See Nancy Pearcey, *Total Truth: Liberating Christianity From Its Cultural Captivity* (Wheaton, IL: Crossway Books, 2004).

[7] Michael Polanyi elaborated these concepts in his books *Personal Knowledge: Towards a Post-Critical Philosophy* (Chicago: University of Chicago Press, 1958, 1962) and *The Tacit Dimension* (Garden City, NY: Doubleday, 1966).

[8] See Brian J. Walsh and J. Richard Middleton, *The Transforming Vision: Shaping a Christian World View* (Downers Grove, IL: InterVarsity Press, 1984).

[9] In *The Universe Next Door: A Basic Worldview Catalogue,* 3rd ed. (Downers Grove, IL: InterVarsity Press, 1997), James W. Sire suggests seven worldview questions: What is prime reality—the really real? What is the nature of external reality, that is, the world around us? What is a human being? What happens to a person at death? Why is it possible to know anything at all? How do we know what is right and wrong? What is the meaning of human history?

[10] In addition, the unpredictable gods of pagan cultures could not provide the cause-and-effect relationship essential for science. See Ariel A. Roth, *Science Finds God* (Hagerstown, MD: Autumn House, 2008).

[11] In *The Tao of Physics: An Exploration of the Parallels Between Modern Physics and Eastern Mysticism* (1975), Fritjof Capra asserts that physics and metaphysics are interconnected.

[12] Paul Kurtz (b. 1925) has been a preeminent spokesman of this worldview perspective through his many books, including *A Secular Humanist Declaration* (1980) and *In Defense of Secular Humanism* (1983), and as editor of *Humanist Manifestos I and II* (1984).

[13] See Steve Wilkens and Mark L. Sanford, *Hidden Worldviews: Eight Cultural Stories That Shape Our Lives* (Downers Grove, IL: IVP Academic, 2009).

[14] See Leonard Brand, *Faith, Reason, and Earth History: A Paradigm of Earth and Biological Origins by Intelligent Design,* 2nd ed. (Berrien Springs, MI: Andrews University Press, 2009).

Chapter 2

What Is Creation Theory?

Many theories have been advanced to explain how the world and life on it came into existence. Most theories of origins can be classified into either creation theories or evolution theories. The theory that will be described here is a creation theory because it assumes supernatural agency in creation, an event actualized by processes that lie beyond our experience. This contrasts with evolution theories postulating that our world originated by gradual processes that are to some degree ongoing. Theistic evolution affirms that gradual evolutionary development is due to supernatural activity.

More specifically, the theory described below belongs to a category commonly known as recent, six-day creation. Several creation theories have been proposed, including the gap theory, day-age theory, and various theories of multiple creations over long ages. Our theory differs from these other creation theories in that it postulates a single, recent, creation of life on earth in six days. It is this theory that is most commonly referred to when terms such as "creation" or "creationists"[1] are employed. The major variation among theories of recent, six-day creation, lies in scope—whether the creation includes the entire universe or only a portion of it. This point will be discussed later.

The biblical basis of creation theory

Creation is a supernatural process, which means the events and processes of creation cannot be discovered through empirical research but must be supernaturally revealed or remain unknown. Thus, we must turn to the Bible to identify the key concepts in this theory. Genesis 1 and 2 provide the major creation texts, although the creation theme is interwoven throughout the Bible, forming the logical basis for the biblical worldview and the salvation story. The approach taken here can be compared with that of others who have identified the major features of the recent, six-day creation theory.[2]

Creator of heaven and earth

Creation starts with God, who was present at the beginning of the universe. Genesis 1 begins with the statement, "In the beginning God created the heavens and the earth." Other texts refer to the presence of the Creator God in the beginning. For example, John 1:1–3 states, "In the beginning was the Word. . . . All things were made by him" (KJV). Other texts making the same point include Psalm 90:1, 2; Proverbs 8:22–31; and Revelation 14:7, among others. A marked contrast is made between the eternal God and the temporal physical universe created by Him.

Creation by fiat

The Creation story of Genesis 1 includes a series of statements indicating that creation occurred in response to God's spoken utterance. According to this passage of the Bible, God says, "Let there be light" and light appears (verse 3, KJV). Similar statements are found throughout Genesis 1. Creation by fiat, or verbal command, is an integral part of a recent, six-day creation, and is attested in other scriptures (e.g., Psalm 33:6, 9; Psalm 148:5; 2 Corinthians 4:6).

Creation by fiat is not the only method God employs. Genesis 1:26 records God as saying, "Let us make man in our image" (KJV); however, the text doesn't indicate whether man was created by verbal command or physical action. In Genesis 2:7, we are told God "formed" man from the ground, implying direct physical effort. Creation through physical action might also be true of some other creation events, although the text does not seem to require it. In some cases, verbal command and direct physical action might be combined in an act of creation. In all cases, however, creation is described as being accomplished by a Divine Agent acting through supernatural processes lying beyond our experience.

A six-day creation

The creation events described in Genesis 1 are arranged in a series of six days, followed by a seventh day of rest—God's Sabbath. Each of the creation days consists of an evening and a morning, indicating the "days" are regular days rather than indefinite periods. Textual support for a six-day creation includes two direct quotes from God Himself (Exodus 20:8–11; 31:17). In addition, many textual allusions affirm the Creation story. Some (e.g., Acts 4:24; 14:15; Revelation 10:6; 14:6–7) repeat specific language from Exodus 20:8–11. Others (e.g., 2 Corinthians 4:6; Hebrews 4:4; 1 Corinthians 11:8–9; Mark 10:6–9) allude to the description of creation in Genesis 1 and 2. Collectively, these texts strongly affirm the veracity of the Genesis record of a six-day creation followed by a Sabbath rest day. The historicity of the creation days is an integral part of a recent, six-day creation theory.

Special creation of humans

Humans have a special place in both the Creation narrative and the Bible as a whole. Humans were uniquely created in God's image (Genesis 1:26, 27). No other creatures are described as having been created in God's likeness. As if to emphasize the uniqueness of humans, Genesis 2 describes how God created Adam—from the dust—and how Adam received life—from God's "breath." Another unique feature is that Adam and Eve were created individually, then joined in marriage; this reminds one of the individuality and union of the Trinity. The uniqueness of humans is noted in other passages (e.g., Genesis 9:6; Psalm 8; James 3:9). The special creation of humans is perhaps the clearest single point that distinguishes creation theories from evolutionary theories.

Good original creation later corrupted

At four points in the Creation narrative of Genesis 1, God states that what He had made was good. In Genesis 1:31, at the end of the sixth day, God declares everything He made was very good. Other biblical texts provide additional details on the kind of world God would describe as good. Revelation 21 and 22 describe a future world in which there is no death or suffering, where the tree of life preserves life indefinitely, as implied in Genesis 3:22. The goodness of the creation implies that evil was not present at that point. Evil was an intruder that did not enter the world until Adam and Eve disbelieved God and disobeyed Him, as described in Genesis 3. With this act of rebellion, evil came into the world in the form of death (Genesis 3:19; Romans 5:12–14; 6:23), and Satan's influence was evident in the world (described in Job 1 and 2 and noted by Jesus in John 12:31; 14:30; and 16:11). Sin brought a curse upon the earth (Genesis 3:17), plants (Genesis 3:18), and animals (Genesis 3:14), but it will eventually be removed (Revelation 22:3). Even though the newly created world was flawless, it was not necessarily complete in every aspect. There was still to be opportunity for future growth and development (Genesis 1:28; 2:15). The principle of a newly created world that was flawless, though not necessarily complete, is an important part of creation theory.

Original created diversity, but not fixity of species

The Creation narrative describes a diversity of created life. The creation of plants included plants bearing seed and fruit trees (Genesis 1:11). Two categories are included here, the herb and the fruit tree, implying diversity. Creatures of the air and water are created on the fifth day, with many types of water creatures and birds (Genesis 1:21). Similarly, the land animals created on the sixth day included cattle, creeping organisms, and beasts of the earth, each with a plurality of kinds (Genesis 1:24, 25). Each was given the power to reproduce, bringing forth offspring distinct from the offspring of other kinds. Some creationists have sought support in these texts for the Greek idea of fixity of species, but nothing in the text implies that the animals would not change. In fact, Genesis 3:14–19 and 6:5–12 clearly indicate that changes have occurred among the animals. Although the idea of original diversity of plants and animals is an important concept in creation theory, the idea of unchanging species is not.

A recent creation of all life on earth

Bible writers do not discuss the date for creation, nor is any theological significance attached to the earth's age. Different chronologies are presented in ancient manuscripts, and no biblical text attempts to provide a total figure. The best-known estimate for creation, roughly six thousand years, is based on the Masoretic text. The Septuagint's figures suggest some seventy-five hundred years. Because of textual uncertainties, potential gaps in the genealogies, and lack of emphasis on a specific date, many creationists prefer to say the creation is likely less than ten thousand years old. The uncertainties allow for some differences in view on the time elapsed since the six-day Creation; however, there is not enough leeway to encompass millions of years. Some scholars have proposed humans existed on earth prior to the Genesis Creation—the so-called "pre-Adamites." This does not harmonize with Jesus' statement in Mark 10:6–9 referring to the creation of Adam and Eve at the "beginning," nor is it supported anywhere in Scripture. The important point here is that the history of life in our world is much shorter than claimed by those adopting a naturalistic worldview.

The scope of creation

Many biblical texts emphasize that God created all that exists (John 1:1–3; Isaiah 44:24). However, the book of Job hints that God may have fashioned other worlds before He made this one. Furthermore, biblical prophecy indicates His plans to create a new world. Thus, we should not assume that the entire universe was formed during the six-day Creation period. Job 38:4–7 suggests the "sons of God" already existed when God formed this world. These may be the same "sons of God" mentioned in Job 1:6 and 2:1.

The Bible writers do not make an issue of whether the universe was created before or during the six-day Creation, and it is not a crucial part of the model described here.[3] However, the possibility that the universe and angels were created previously introduces some interesting implications. First, it provides an explanation for Satan's origin and his subsequent fall before Adam and Eve's rebellion. (A brief history of Satan is found in Isaiah 14 and Ezekiel 28 and is alluded to by Jesus in Luke 10:18.) It seems unlikely that a perfect Lucifer living in a sinless universe would rebel immediately after his creation. Second, a previously created universe might explain the absence of any record of the creation of water during the six days of creation. The Creation description begins with a planet that is dark, wet, and uninhabited (Genesis 1:2; see also 2 Peter 3:5). This would be perfectly understandable if the planet had been created earlier, with God choosing at some point to make it habitable for the humans He planned to create. There should be no theological or philosophical objections to either of these possibilities, since the Bible indicates God will create again (Revelation 21 and 22) and many parts of the present creation, including Venus and Mars, remain uninhabited.

Global catastrophe

A global flood is described in Genesis chapters 6–9, and is affirmed by allusions and references in Isaiah 54:9; Hebrews 11:7; 1 Peter 3:20;

2 Peter 3:5, 6; and by Jesus' own comments in Matthew 24:37–39. The Flood is not, strictly speaking, an element of the Creation story, but it does relate to the fossil sequence, which is often used to argue against the six-day Creation. The Flood provides the explanatory connection between the Creation week and the geologic column. There is no need to postulate long periods of time to produce the geologic column if it was produced in a global catastrophe. Thus, the idea of a global flood properly belongs in a discussion of creation theory.

Conclusion

The creation theory outlined here is based on a direct reading of the Bible as an account of God's actions in the creation of earth. The Bible is historically reliable, divinely guided in its production, and written in everyday language. It is not a science textbook with detailed descriptions of physical mechanisms identifying cause and effect; however, it does accurately reveal some of the ways God acted in the Creation. Since Creation was a supernatural process, it would be inappropriate to test the veracity of the Genesis account using a naturalistic methodology such as science.[4]

Our purpose here has been to identify those elements in the Creation narrative that are given emphasis in Scripture, and to incorporate them into a theory of biblical creation. The most important features of the Creation account include God's eternal nature as contrasted with the temporality of the material universe; the effective power of God's verbal commands in creation; a six-day creation including living organisms and their physical environment; the unique creation of humans in God's image; the unflawed condition of the original creation before the entrance of evil; the origination of diverse forms of living organisms during the Creation week; and finally, a global catastrophe that destroyed most living organisms and altered the surface of the world.

L. James Gibson is currently director of the Geoscience Research Institute, with major interests in historical biology and in the relationship of creation and science. After completing his BA and MA degrees at Pacific Union College, he taught secondary school science and mathematics in California and in West Africa. Further graduate work led to a PhD in biology from Loma Linda University in 1984, when he joined the Geoscience Research Institute, becoming its director in 1994. He has written several articles and chapters for a number of journals and books, has participated in numerous seminars on faith and science on six continents, and is editor of the journal Origins.

References

[1] For example, R. L. Numbers, *The Creationists* (Berkeley, CA: University of California Press, 1992); "Creationism" in http://en.wikipedia.org/wiki/Creationism; T. A. McIver, *Creationism: Intellectual Origins, Cultural Context, and Theoretical Diversity,* PhD dissertation, University of California at Los Angeles (Ann Arbor, MI: University Microfilms International, 1989).

[2] The most concise account is B. R. Neufeld, "Towards the Development of a General Theory of Creation," *Origins* 1 (1974): 6–13. Other descriptions of creation include H. G. Coffin, R. H. Brown, and L. J. Gibson, *Origin by Design* (Hagerstown, MD: Review and Herald Publishing Association, 2005); A. A. Roth, *Origins: Linking Science and Scripture* (Hagerstown, MD: Review and Herald, 1998); P. Nelson and J. M. Reynolds, "Young Earth Creationism," in *Three Views on Creation and Evolution,* J. P. Moreland and J. M. Reynolds, eds. (Grand Rapids, MI: Zondervan, 1999), 41–75; K. P. Wise, *Faith, Form, and Time* (Nashville, TN: Broadman and Holman Publishers, 2002).

[3] Some scholars consider the wording of Genesis 1:16 with reference to the stars to be a parenthetical reference that God is also the Creator of the stars, without specifying when they were created. Some scholars would include the entire universe in the Creation week, while others would interpret the passage to mean that some portion of the starry universe was created at that time. Ambiguities in the Hebrew wording make it difficult to be dogmatic on this point.

[4] There is ample empirical evidence for the existence of a Divine Creator, as seen in the order and design of the universe and of life. However, the specifics of how creation took place can only be known by special revelation.

—2

Chapter 3

Are the Bible and Science in Conflict?

In discussions of science and faith, one often gets the impression that either science or Scripture can be believed—not both. In the secular world, science is by default seen as the true source of knowledge. The Bible, if considered at all, is seen as useful only as a source of spiritual insight—as long as it presents no conflict to the current scientific consensus. This chapter will examine the question: Are the Bible and science in conflict? Then we will explore how a believer who is also a scientist can relate to the issue.[1]

Before proceeding, let us define what is meant by "science" in this chapter. By "science" I refer to a systematic process that attempts to explain phenomena in terms of the physical mechanisms that cause them. Other definitions are possible, but this definition will suffice for our purposes. In a similar vein, a miracle is an event that cannot be explained solely by naturalistic scientific means.

Experimental and historical sciences

In discussing science and faith, it is useful to distinguish between experimental (or empirical) science on the one hand and historical science on the other. Sciences that are mainly experimental (e.g., chemistry, physics, anatomy, ecology) involve the manipulation of physical conditions in order to isolate and identify causal factors that will explain an event. Those sciences that are mainly historical (e.g., archaeology, paleontology) study the results of some past event and attempt to explain what occurred in order to produce the observed evidence.

Most sciences include both empirical and historical aspects. However, only the empirical aspects are open for experimentation—the historical parts are not. Normally, there is no conflict between Scripture and experimental science. Difficulties arise when attempting to understand historical events for which the Bible provides a supernatural explanation, while a scientist attempts to arrive at a naturalistic explanation.

Different types of Bible passages

Before considering further the ways in which science and Scripture seem difficult to reconcile, let us note that there are many areas where we find no conflict. For example, although the Bible is not primarily a science text, it nevertheless describes many phenomena of a scientific nature. Various Bible authors mention mammals, birds, and plants. Aspects of anatomy, physiology, and behavior—plant, animal, and human—are mentioned by Bible authors. The Bible describes the creation of life forms, implying that God designed and fabricated the living systems available for us to study today. Science today confirms the appearance of design at all levels of complexity, although considerable disagreement exists over the cause of the design.

Some passages in the Bible were written in symbolic terms or in figures of speech. Thus, one might mistakenly interpret an expression as literal when it is in fact figurative. For example, Habakkuk 3:3 says that God came from Teman. Perhaps some people would conclude from that text that God lives in Teman but most of us consider this to be a figure of speech. Here, God is represented as coming from the south, or Sinai where the Ten Commandments were given. Other passages may be poetic, illustrative, or expressions of common understanding not written to convey scientific explanations. On the other hand, there are many passages of Scripture that are clearly intended as historical narrative. These include passages such as Genesis 1–11, the Gospel accounts of Jesus' miracles, and His virgin birth, death, and resurrection. The clearly expository prose does not support attempts to "spiritualize" them or otherwise categorize them as figurative, poetic, etc.

Natural and supernatural explanations

We are able to offer two possible explanations of phenomena (or events): natural or supernatural. The two explanatory systems may be in conflict or may complement each other. As the Bible primarily describes God's activities in the course of human history, it almost always proffers supernatural explanations. As mentioned above, explanations of past events are inherently not directly testable by scientific methods. For a given phenomena that the Bible describes as supernatural, a materialistic (or naturalistic) scientist may give a naturalistic explanation. In some instances, both explanations may apply. In other words, God may well have used ordinary physical processes in a supernatural way to accomplish His will.

Many of the great scientists of the past were believers and saw no conflict between the Bible and science. In the seventeenth century, scientists were divided into two camps in regard to religion and science (or philosophy, as it was then called). Francis Bacon and Galileo Galilei belonged to the "separatist" group who felt that the Book of Scripture and the Book of Nature were best kept separate, while recognizing that both had the same Author.[2] In the past half-century, American scientist Stephen Gould has extended the idea of separation with his NOMA (Nonoverlapping Magisteria) proposal, which declared science and religion occupy separate realms that do not interact.[3] According to Gould, religion deals with spiritual and ethical ideas while science deals with the real world. Accepting NOMA thus seems to necessitate rejection of Scripture as the inspired Word of God. The other group of seventeenth-century scientists, the Pansophists, viewed science and Scripture as being ultimately in harmony.

Thus, both groups arrived at a "no conflict" answer—the separatists because they compartmentalized the fields of study, and the Pansophists because they saw science as reinforcing Scripture. Both groups saw God as Author of Scripture and Creator of the world. Any apparent conflict lay in a disagreement between interpretations of the Bible and/or interpretations of science. We might take the same approach today with one additional caveat—not all of our questions will be answered. Since we are in a sinful world and have only incomplete understanding of science and Scripture, we will not arrive at complete answers to all questions.

Areas of conflict

Conflict is especially prominent in the study of origins, which is a historical question, not an experimental one. Those with a naturalistic worldview prefer evolutionary theory because it posits explanations in terms of purely physical mechanisms. Those with a worldview based on biblical revelation prefer creation theory because it accepts biblical accounts of supernatural activity in the creation and maintenance of the natural world. Both views appeal to evidence. Because that evidence is so incomplete and open to different explanation, the scientist's worldview comes to play a major role in interpretation. We will now turn to areas where conflict is very much in evidence.

One of the best known examples is found in Galileo Galilei (1564–1642), considered by many to be the father of modern observational astronomy, modern physics, and ultimately the individual most responsible for the birth of modern science.

In the late sixteenth century, leaders of the Roman Catholic Church endorsed the idea that the earth was the center of the universe. While a pious believer, Galileo was nevertheless a scientist. He advocated Copernicus' idea that the earth revolved around the sun. Since the church considered itself the supreme authority, Galileo was deemed a heretic.[4] In this example, it is important to note that Galileo's problem was not strictly a Bible/science conflict, but reflected a difference between religious leaders and some scientists over how to interpret the Bible and scientific data.

In the eyes of most materialistic scientists, conflict has always existed between secular scientists and those who hold a theistic worldview. Books have been written on the topic of the so-called "war" between "science and religion."[5] Unfortunately, overzealous Christians share in the responsibility for this conflict. Serious thinkers were often alienated by superstition, suppression, and coercion (associated with the dominant church), and this led to distrust of the Bible itself.

The Bible chronicles the occurrence of numerous miracles, which are almost invariably interpreted differently by two groups. A person not persuaded of the Bible's divine inspiration (i.e., a "nonbeliever" in this discussion) concludes that the miracle did not in fact occur and that the biblical account is fallacious. The nonbeliever arrives at one of the following conclusions: (1) the writer *thought* it happened the way he wrote it but was wrong; (2) he knew it was wrong but was trying to fool his audience; or (3) he wanted to make a point and merely told an illustrative story to do so. In any of these cases, the biblical report is regarded as unreliable, or at the least, not to be taken literally. In contrast, the person who accepts the Bible as divinely inspired (a "believer" in this discussion), accepts the miracle by faith. Because the occurrence was placed in the Bible, and the Bible is God's Word, the believer accepts that God used His power to cause the miracle.

Miracles with no available physical evidence

Now we will turn our attention to miracles for which we have no physical evidence. An example included by Gospel writers is Jesus walking on the water (see Matthew 14:25–32). Skeptics might suggest that Jesus may have known the location of rocks just under the surface so that He could walk from land to the boat, thus appearing to walk on water. Peter, not knowing the location of these rocks, lost his footing and had to be rescued. Believers may rightfully regard such explanations as strained, but since no direct physical evidence is available to us today, we cannot conduct any test. Thus, we either accept or reject the story based on our personal presuppositions.

A second example is Jairus' daughter, a young girl who has died, whom Jesus brings back to life (see Luke 8:49–56). The nonbeliever may observe that Jesus Himself declared the girl was only asleep (Matthew 9:24), and that He merely awoke her. Matthew's and Luke's reports are thus discounted as wrong. We have no direct physical evidence to know for sure whether the girl was in fact dead or not. One's response to the account will depend on one's confidence in the reliability of Scripture.

Miracles with physical effects observable to us

Miracles for which physical evidence does exist today seem to present more problematic issues. At times, it appears that scientific evidence strongly disagrees with our most careful interpretation of Scripture. These are issues that we might call "No conflict, but . . ." issues. Our belief is that the Bible and science are not in conflict. Nevertheless, they do appear to be so. To resolve these issues, evidence must be very carefully evaluated, as it can be interpreted in many different ways.

According to a believer, the origin of life on earth is an example of a miraculous event in which the Bible and science are not in conflict. For more than half a century, numerous experiments have been conducted in an attempt to produce life from nonliving material via naturalistic means. Thus far, these experiments have failed to produce empirical evidence for the spontaneous origin of life. Therefore the believer feels this is consistent with the biblical narration that life originated through supernatural activity. The nonbeliever would not be convinced—the absence of evidence is not seen to constitute good evidence. The fact that organic molecules have been made from inorganic gases is taken by secular scientists as evidence that spontaneous generation of a living cell could occur and therefore there is conflict in their minds.

The area where the "No conflict, but . . ." questions are perhaps the most vexing is the amount of time required for accumulation of the fossil-bearing sediments in the earth's crust. There seems to be a conflict between the relatively short time implied in the Bible and the long time inferred by science. Ice cores offer another example. In places on the world's surface like Greenland, a thick layer of ice has formed. When the ice is drilled into and a core is pulled out, one sees that there are different layers, like rings in a tree. Some ice cores may contain 160,000 layers,[6] the lower ones which have been identified by chemical means. Since the layers are presumably laid down one layer each year, this presents a conflict with the Bible's timetable. Of course, there are no dates in the Bible, but most conservative biblical scholars have used genealogies mentioned in the text to conclude that not much more than ten thousand years are represented by biblical history.

Many other examples can be given of conventional dating techniques that suggest the earth is much older than ten thousand years. Many Bible-believing scientists see no conflict in old dates for rocks. God certainly could have created the rocks of the earth many millions of years ago and then organized the earth's crust during a more recent Creation week. However, there are many examples of fossils found in rocks dated by standard techniques as much older than ten thousand years.

Even considering these problems, we have evidence that the last chapter in age dating has not yet been written. In some cases, new scientific evidence may cast doubt on current conventional age dating. For example, soft tissue was recently discovered inside fossil dinosaur bones thought to be about sixty-seven million years old.[7] No one has a good idea to explain how soft tissue can survive that long. Another example is the discovery of the catastrophic nature of the Yellowstone fossil forests,[8] once thought to represent long ages of ordinary processes. Other evidence for rapid deposition of sediments includes the rapid underwater deposition of turbidites (geological formation that were caused by a type of underwater avalanche) and the rates of erosion of the continents, which seems to be too rapid for the supposed great age of the earth.[9]

Taking the Bible as myth creates more problems

Some people solve the conflict by concluding that the biblical miracles are myths—traditional stories that serve to express a worldview. For these individuals, no conflict exists since the event didn't happen the way it was described. For example, there really wasn't a man named Daniel who spent the night in a lions' den. This is merely a story told to show that God takes care of those who believe in Him.

However, this approach undermines the inspiration of Scripture. Some people see the ages obtained by conventional dating as so strongly indicating an old earth that they conclude a literal reading of the Bible to be absurd. Such individuals may accept the ideas of some biblical scholars who believe that parts of Genesis (chapter 1, for example) were written after other sections. If we take this view of Scripture, we might well end up denying Christ's life and ministry. The evidence against the bodily resurrection of Christ is comparable to that against a literal reading of Genesis 1.

If we are going to be consistent in our understanding of the inspiration of Scripture, we need to be ready to accept that miracles did occur and that, using conventional means, we cannot prove how they happened. Thus the conflict remains.

Conflict may be unavoidable in some cases

For most believers, it is no surprise for there to be conflict between faith and secular science. Christian doctrines are based on faith, and are supported by evidence that appeals to reason, including personal experience, documentary evidence, and eye witness testimonies. Empirical evidence is also important but is not the only factor as it is in secular science.

When interpreting Scripture, we must always do so in humility. Are there other interpretations possible that do not destroy the original meaning? We may accept alternate views if the passage allows for them, while not losing sight of the event's miraculous nature. The same principle should apply to interpreting science—a humble attitude and consideration of alternative hypotheses. Maintaining this attitude can help keep conflicts between the Bible and science in perspective.

If we are consistent in our understanding of Scripture's inspiration, we must be ready to accept that miraculous events did in fact occur and that, using conventional means, we cannot prove how they happened. Thus, the potential for conflict remains—as it will as long as the world does, in its present iteration.

Conclusion

Perhaps God will someday reveal to us the kind of science He employs, the laws within which He has chosen to operate. Only then will we understand that there was no conflict after all. For the present, we must live with the tension, which for a scientist, can at times be considerable.

From the above, we can conclude that there will always be some conflict between science and the Bible. Some apparent conflicts may be resolved as science makes new discoveries, but others will only be resolved in eternity. Conflict between the Bible and science arises for several reasons including: (1) differing philosophical understandings of the role of God in nature; (2) the difficulty of interpreting the history of the world scientifically; (3) the inability of science to explain in scientific terms what God did miraculously; and (4) the brevity and incompleteness of the biblical information about the history of nature.

All of these questions and conflicts should present opportunities for scientists and theologians to grow together in their understanding. The tragedy is that both often seem limited by and locked into their own perspective and fail to communicate in a common language.

David B. Ekkens earned his BA and MA degrees from Andrews University and then taught secondary school for four years. He received his PhD in biology from Loma Linda University and taught at Southwestern Adventist College (now Southwestern Adventist University) for two years. He then traveled to Africa to teach for four years in Nigeria and for six years at the University of Eastern Africa in Kenya. This was followed by one year of postdoctoral studies in the neurophysiology lab at Andrews University. He joined the science faculty at Kettering College of Medical Arts before moving to Southern Adventist University, from which he recently retired.

References

[1] For helpful suggestions on how to deal with tension, see chapter 20 by Burdick in this volume.

[2] F. E. Manuel, *The Religion of Isaac Newton* (London: Oxford University Press, 1973).

[3] Stephen Jay Gould, "Nonoverlapping Magisteria," *Natural History* 106 (1997): 16–22.

[4] Maurice A. Finocchiaro, "Myth 8. That Galileo Was Imprisoned and Tortured for Advocating Copernicanism," in *Galileo Goes to Jail and Other Myths About Science and Religion,* R. L. Numbers, ed. (London: Harvard University Press, 2009), 68–78.

[5] William H. Jennings, *Storms Over Genesis: Biblical Battleground in America's Wars of Religion* (Minneapolis, MN: Fortress Press, 2007).

[6] T. H. Jacka, "Antarctic Ice Cores and Environmental Change," Glaciology Program, Antarctic Cooperative Research Centre and Australian Antarctic Division, http://www.chem.hope .edu/~polik/warming/IceCore/IceCore2.html (accessed March 11, 2010).

[7] M. H. Schweitzer et al., "Analyses of Soft Tissue From *Tyrannosaurus Rex* Suggest the Presence of Protein," *Science* 316, no. 5822 (2007): 277–280.

[8] H. Coffin, "The Puzzle of the Petrified Trees," *Dialogue* 4, no. 1 (1992): 11–13, 30, 31. Also available online at http://www.aiias.edu/ict/vol_08/08cc_091-095.htm#_ednref6.

[9] A. A. Roth, *Origins: Linking Science and Scripture* (Hagerstown, MD: Review and Herald, 1998).

Chapter 4

What Is the Difference Between Data and Interpretation?

Consider the following statements.

Statement 1: A is a human being. B is a gorilla. There are many similarities between A and B, but A has many superior attributes compared to B.

Statement 2: The similarities show that A and B had a common origin—evolution. The superiorities indicate that A evolved more progressively than B since their divergence from a common ancestor.

Statement 3: The similarities show that A and B had a common origin—creation. The superior attributes of A indicate that God created humans in His own image. This was not the case with the creation of animals.

Statement 4: The similarities show that A and B had a common origin—creation. The superior attributes of A indicate that God directed the evolution of A. God may or may not have directed the evolutionary path of animals subsequent to their creation.

Statement 1 is data—observable, knowable, and open to experience. Statements 2, 3, and 4 are interpretations of facts—one by an evolutionist, one by a creationist, and one by a theistic evolutionist.

This illustration reveals that knowledge or information can be divided into two separate concepts: data and interpretation. Since data are subject to interpretation, both researchers and nonscientists must distinguish between the information constituting the collected data and the "information" derived from the data that is presented as evidence in support of a hypothesis.

Although scientists endeavor to be objective, certain factors (biases) influence selection and interpretation of data. The information provided to the general public is often more interpretation than data. For this reason, it is essential for us to develop and apply critical thinking skills.

Knowing the difference

What do we mean by "data"? What are the differences between data and interpretation? Data consist of measurements and observations used as a basis for reasoning, discussion, or calculation.[1] While observable data are usually regarded as unalterable facts, they may or may not be true. As technology and science progress, "facts" are discarded, modified, or replaced with new data. For example, measurements may form a basis for identification (an interpretation) of an object or phenomenon. Fossils of extinct organisms are often identified based on measurements of body parts that have been preserved. The accuracy and precision of the measurements make correct identification difficult because with many of the extinct fauna, scientists don't know whether or not large organisms with similar structure to small organisms represent different species, developmental stages, or gender. The actual identifications or calculations are not data—they are interpretations. Much of the controversy in the scientific literature occurs because interpretations are drawn from limited databases.

The complexity of data and interpretations

As an illustration of the complex interplay between data and interpretations, consider two steps involved in the process of merely identifying rocks and minerals.

Step 1. Interpretations of light properties of minerals.

Light properties of minerals are described from the microscopic examination of a very thin slice of rock (a "thin section"). Polarized light (light waves vibrating in only one plane) is used to conduct tests on the light properties of each mineral in the thin section. The tests provide a visual database of light's transmission patterns. Mineralogists use these patterns to determine the sample's composition. Identification of the minerals is an interpretation based on the light property data.

Step 2. Determination of rock type.

Rock type can be determined by examining the contact of one mineral with another and measuring how much of each mineral is present. A geologist who identifies the rock considers the mineral identifications "data" even though the identification is actually an interpretation of an interpretation. (The mineralogical "data" were originally determined from the light property data.) Thus, the scope of what constitutes data is actually quite narrow.

Just how valid is identification? Identifications can be made using comparisons with standards. For example, three thin sections may have the same mineral composition but the mineral contacts may be very different. If the mineral grains interlock, the rock is *igneous*. If they are altered, distorted, elongated, and aligned, it is *metamorphic rock*. The same minerals cemented together form *sedimentary rock*.

When terms and procedures are well defined, identification is fairly easy and relatively reliable. However, since "data" are limited to what we can measure or directly observe, we must take care in its interpretation in order to reach reliable conclusions. An interpretation is an explanation, and interpretations are limited by the availability of data and the bias of the observer.

Multiple levels of interpretation

Several levels of interpretation exist. For example, the term *oolite* not only identifies a rock type but also implies an entire history of environmental requirements and depositional conditions for its formation. How can a simple term carry that much interpretative information?

First, a thin section of round, beadlike particles cemented together must be identified with respect to its mineralization. The first level of interpretation is to identify the mineral composition of the little beads. For the purposes of this illustration, let's identify them as particles of calcium carbonate.

Identification of the structure of the round, bead-filled rock is based on recognition of a central object, for example a piece of some other kind of rock or a bit of shell material around which the calcium carbonate has precipitated. This structural information coupled with the roundness of the particles identifies the beads as oolites. At this point, one might think that identification has concluded. However, a third level of interpretation is introduced to explain how the oolites were formed.

The third level relies on observations of current environments. Geologists know that oolites are typically formed near a shore by the agitation of warm, shallow, saline waters and apply this knowledge to oolitic rocks found on a mountainside. In other words, geologists assume that the mountain oolites formed at that site sometime in the past in the same way that oolites form in the ocean or Utah's Great Salt Lake. This interpretation implies that oolites don't form in any other way. The reasoning seems logical; however, this association may not be true. This set of interpretations is now added to other data with multiple interpretations bringing us to the final description of a particular rock exposure or outcrop.

Geologists use other rock types and additional data to develop models to describe geologic events in earth's history. For example, cemented quartz grains are called sandstones. Patterns in sandstone may be due to the process of cross-bedding. Typically, cross-beds are formed as currents (wind and/or water) deposit sand and silt on the lee slope of dunes. By integrating regional data and interpretations, geologists develop the fourth level of interpretation—modeling. Models provide scientists with a generalized framework for developing predictions and assessing events that may have occurred in the past.[2]

Thus, when evaluating research, it is essential to make the distinction between data and interpretation. The validity of an interpretation is based on how well it accommodates available data. Interpretations may change as the database changes. This interplay between data and interpretations is what makes science so successful and progressive.

Bias during data acquisition

Scientists are aware they are subject to error and misconception; however, they try to maintain an objective attitude.[3] This commitment has created a sort of aura around scientists. People often prefer to believe that scientists deal with absolutes. Some even think that when a scientist draws a conclusion, all questions have been resolved and competing theories refuted. To complicate matters, the scientific community has adopted the position that any researcher having a religious bias is nonscientific; therefore, by definition, creation-science cannot be true science. Such an attitude fails to recognize its own bias.[4]

Here are some biases that influence science—some technical, some subtle and unconscious factors.

1. *Sampling constraints.* The first problem in data-gathering is sampling bias. Every scientist has some preconceived ideas about the research that influences the selection of data. Various sampling methods help minimize problems,[5] but even then, choices may favor a particular hypothesis.

2. *Systematic errors.* The scientist may have a "blind spot"—a failure to recognize data. For example, it is common for a paleontologist

specializing in fossil snails to collect a wider variety of gastropods than anyone else at a site. However, that same individual will have fewer clams and corals. These fossils could significantly impact the scientist's interpretation, but the researcher's bias eliminates that input. Furthermore, the processing of data can introduce systematic bias.[6] An unrecognized faulty procedure or an incorrectly applied mathematical formula or statistical analysis introduces a systematic error or bias into the results.

3. *Technological constraints.* Scientists can now incorporate large quantities of data and interpretations into computer-generated models through analyses involving pattern recognition. However, gigantic databases do not necessarily mean that models adequately reflect complex systems and processes. The development of simplified models with computer-generated systems produces technological bias because the simplified parameters place limits on the application of the model to real systems.[7]

4. *Quality of data.* Analysis of data introduces bias due to the inclusion of qualitative or subjective interpretations. For example, in the analysis of potassium-argon data, the quantity of potassium and argon can be measured very precisely. However, it is difficult to know just what that data mean, and the conclusions relative to age depend heavily on numerous assumptions.[8] Current technology does not measure the age of the rock directly, thus the conclusions drawn are interpretations. Descriptive data are even more problematic.

5. *Financial constraints.* Scientific method requires rigorous testing before any theory can be accepted. However, time and monetary constraints increase technical bias by limiting the experimental process. New data are incorporated into current theory because it is easier to get material published if it is generally accepted by the scientific community. The funding process has an incredible influence on research today.[9] The rigorous testing proposed by the scientific method is not cost-effective, so ideas and concepts are rushed into print, then cited as evidence in subsequent publications.

Implications for science and religion

When it comes to the interface between science and religion, several points need to be noted. First, not all data are accurately measured, and it is sometimes hard to differentiate between data and interpretation. Multiple, alternative interpretations of any database are not only possible but probable, although the simplest theoretical scenario is usually preferred over the more complex one. Second, bias is present in any interpretation because all scientific interpretations are at least partly subjective. Third, we must understand the nature of science and how scientists work. People sometimes get discouraged because scientific interpretations seem to be constantly changing—they're not sure what to believe. However, that is the nature of science and how it advances. Once one grasps this aspect of science, one is reluctant to base theological beliefs on specific data or scientific concepts. Fourth, while science may provide relevant information, it should not dictate theology. If it is allowed to do so, then every time scientific interpretations change, theology has to alter, whether or not that alteration is consistent with one's belief system and experiences. At the same time, theology should not dictate anyone's science. Concepts such as "fixity of species" held by many in the seventeenth and eighteenth centuries,[10] and the belief in a "geocentric universe" are some ideas that contributed to conflict between science and theology. The Bible can supply legitimate working hypotheses and constraints for scientific interpretations. In fact, Scripture as an information source points to avenues of investigation that would not be considered by most non-Christian investigators. However, such research should acknowledge any scriptural bias present and all the data must be fairly evaluated.

Nevertheless, particularly in the area of origins, science alone cannot assess the complete database. This is because the scientific approach rejects the possibility of supernatural involvement in earth's history. Although some scientists are theistic evolutionists, many scientists believe science and Scripture are simply irreconcilable.[11]

For example, Ayala states, "To claim that the statements of Genesis are scientific truth is to deny all the evidence."[12] Another scientist said, "Not only is the present the key to the past, but the present is the key to the future."[13] Such comments tend to antagonize many Christians in the scientific community. Both the historical accounts of a worldwide Flood and the prophetic accounts of Christ's second advent proclaim the falsity of that concept.[14] The evidence does not prove either a long or short history for life—it simply provides limited information. The data are not the primary problem in reconciling science and Scripture. The primary conflict lies in *interpretation* of the data. For this reason, some believe theistic evolutionists should become the public advocates for evolution. Some hope theistic evolutionists can bridge the gap between science and faith for the general public while marginalizing the creationists.[15]

For many Christians, the historicity of the Bible provides information about creation that suggests a better way to approach science. From this perspective, harmony between science and Scripture may be increased. Working with the same data, creationists expect coherence because they recognize God as Creator of nature and its scientific "laws."

M. Elaine Graham-Kennedy obtained bachelor's degrees in geology and teaching sciences at Phillips University, with further studies at Oklahoma State University. She taught secondary school earth and life sciences in Oklahoma and California. After obtaining a master's degree in geology at Loma Linda University, she completed a PhD in the same field at the University of Southern California. Between 1991 and 2005 she served as a researcher at the Geoscience Research Institute. She authored several book chapters and journal articles on science and faith and published a book for everyone who is young at heart titled Dinosaurs: Where Did They Come From . . . Where Did They Go?

References

[1] *Webster's College Dictionary* (1991).

[2] Andrew D. Miall, *Principles of Sedimentary Basin Analysis* (New York: Springer-Verlag, 1984), 3.

[3] Francisco Ayala et al., *On Being a Scientist* (Washington, DC: National Academy of Sciences Press, 1989), 1.

[4] Del Ratzsch, *The Battle of Beginnings: Why Neither Side Is Winning the Creation–Evolution Debate* (Downers Grove, IL: InterVarsity Press, 1996), 158–179. See also Philip E. Johnson, *Darwin on Trial* (Downers Grove, IL: InterVarsity Press, 1991), 6–12.

[5] Larry Thomas, *Coal Geology* (Chichester, England: John Wiley & Sons Ltd., 2002), 128.

[6] http://www.statistics.com/resources/glossary/s/syse.

[7] Walther Schwarzacher, *Sedimentation Models and Quantitative Stratigraphy* (Amsterdam: Elsevier Scientific Publishing Company, 1975), 1.

[8] C. M. R. Fowler, *The Solid Earth: An Introduction to Global Geophysics* (Cambridge: Cambridge University Press, 1998), 192.

[9] Francisco J. Ayala and Bert Black, "Science and the Courts," *American Scientist* 81 (1993): 230–239.

[10] J. Browne, *The Secular Ark* (New Haven, CT: Yale University Press, 1983), 21–23.

[11] Colin Norman, "Nobelists Unite Against 'Creation Science,'" *Science* 233 (1986): 935.

[12] Ibid.

[13] Alan Baharlou, personal communication from 1978 that echoes sentiment of James Hutton in 1788, "The results, therefore, of our present inquiry is, that we find no vestige of a beginning—no prospect of an end" (*Transactions of the Royal Society of Edinburgh*).

[14] 2 Peter 3:3–10.

[15] Daryl P. Domning, "Winning Their Hearts and Minds: Who Should Speak for Evolution?" *Reports of the National Center for Science Education* 29, no. 2 (2009): 30–32.

Chapter 5

What Is the Evidence for a Creator?

Most people would agree that we exist and that this means that we, and the rest of reality, must have been caused by something. For millennia, humans have pondered what the cause of everything might be, and have arrived at two fundamentally different conclusions.

Ancient Epicureans along with modern Darwinists explain everything to be the result of chance and the intrinsic properties of matter. Cicero summarized Epicurean beliefs this way:

> For he [Epicurus] who taught us all the rest has also taught us that the world was made by nature, without needing an artificer to construct it . . .[1]

The other conclusion is that the world appears to be a product of conscious design and thus requires a Creator to explain its existence. This view permeates Scripture and was summarized by the apostle Paul:

For since the creation of the world God's invisible qualities—his eternal power and divine nature—have been clearly seen, being understood from what has been made, so that men are without excuse.[2]

Bible-believing Christians—along with many Jews, Muslims, Hindus, and others—believe the evident design in nature provides compelling evidence of a Creator.

Evidence for design and the inadequacy of chance

So what evidence of design is there in the creation? The phenomenon of interdependence, which pervades nature, is compelling. Interdependence—in which individual forms elegantly fit functions of a greater whole—is found in everything from the design of the universe to the ways in which organisms interact with other organisms as well as their physical environment. This interdependence found in nature is similar to the interdependence found in my engineer-designed car—an elegant transportation device made from interacting components and constructed of appropriate materials.

There are good reasons that air or water are not the primary materials used in automobile manufacturing. What is true of automobiles is true of life. It, too, is made from just the right stuff—the element carbon. It was once thought that life might just as well be based on other elements, like silicon,[3] but careful consideration of alternative elements reveals that carbon has just the right properties for life. Carbon is made out of just the right subatomic particles and the fundamental forces of the universe have just the right values. The universe itself appears to be just the right kind of universe for life, and our Milky Way just the right kind of galaxy. Our solar system is in just the right location in the Milky Way, and our just-right earth orbits our just-right sun, so that the entire system cooperates for life's existence.[4]

Our apparently mundane gravity impacts multiple factors just right for life to exist. With weaker gravity, earth would lose its atmosphere, while solar nuclear reactions would cease. Alternatively, with stronger gravity, our sun would "burn" hotter, emitting scorching radiation before burning out. There are more reasons gravity is just right, but numerous other factors also render earth life-friendly: abundant water—as unique and as vital as carbon; the moon; earth's tilted axis; water currents pumping equatorial heat into temperate regions—everything comes together elegantly for life on earth, much as the pistons, connecting rods, and other parts of an engine integrate to result in cars that can be driven.

Postulating a naturalistic story to account for engines is possible: metals mixed deep in the earth came together in a fortuitous way deep inside volcanoes to produce engines. It is also possible to generate a naturalistic story explaining our life-friendly universe and earth. However, one philosophical question needing an answer before reasonable conclusions can be drawn involves how many coincidences must occur before something is attributed to design rather than good fortune. Someone winning the lottery is very lucky, but when the lottery administrator's wife wins the lottery 100 percent of the time, good fortune seems a strained explanation.

Without time, space, matter, energy, and anything else that makes up our universe, does chance exist? Attributing the origin of the universe to a chance lottery may be equivalent to rolling a six with no dice. Even with a nature in which chance is possible, chance may still be an unsatisfying explanation for life. Life operates by laws well-suited for its existence and operation, but these same laws of nature seem to preclude life's origin absent outside intervention. For example, life is based on biological macromolecules like proteins and DNA, composed of subunits that are joined together by removal of water molecules. Under reasonable conditions, these "condensation" reactions do not spontaneously occur in water. In fact, radiation, free radicals, and other elements combine with water to break down biological molecules. The only way that life, which is based on carbon and water, can survive is by constantly harnessing energy—mostly from the sun—by utilizing the magnificent set of machinery that performs photosynthesis. Life is a system that uses this energy to continually remake its components. Without a complete interdependent minimal set of molecular machinery, life simply does not happen.

The machinery of life exhibits interdependence in many beautiful ways. In energy metabolism, a central player is a remarkable machine called ATP Synthase (figure 1). It is composed of many interdependent proteins, all precisely fitted together. One part of this molecular machine acts like a turbine, transmitting torque through a "drive shaft" protein to power a "mill" that combines ADP and phosphate to produce ATP, a molecule that serves as the basic energy currency of cells. In other words, ATP Synthase acts like a windmill, harnessing energy to do work. When we see windmills with all of their integrated parts carefully crafted to cooperate in carrying out a task, we immediately recognize machines made by someone who wishes to use natural laws to perform work. Outside of a philosophical need to do otherwise, why would we not recognize design in

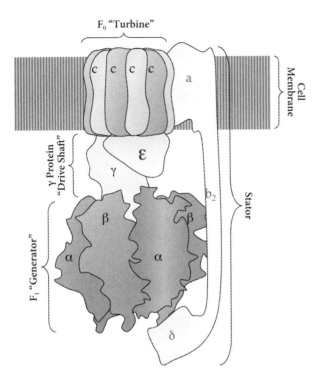

Figure 1. *E. coli* ATP Synthase is similar in principle to ATP Synthase found in other organisms, including humans, although some differences in detail are evident. Arguments may be made about how "reducible" this specific structure is, but clearly the function of the whole is dependent on very specific parts, even though some variation may exist in the parts and overall design.

ATP Synthase and the thousands of other molecular machines inside cells, just as we identify it in windmills? At what point does life "win the lottery" too many times—and without even buying a ticket?

Components of molecular machines are not the end of the interdependence in living things; the machines themselves are interdependent, forming interdependent subcellular systems, a significant number of which are required for life. As organisms increase in complexity there are further levels of interdependence—between different cell types in tissues, between tissues comprising organs, between organs making organ systems, and ultimately organisms themselves. Systems like this would normally be explained as designed. Naturalistic Darwinism invokes natural selection coupled with chance DNA mutations. Such an explanation strains to account for single examples of elegant interdependence, let alone the massive interdependence evident in nature.

Could *all* the interdependence in nature really be produced in small incremental changes filtered through natural selection? The difference between insect compound eyes and human camera-type eyes is as profound as the difference between piston and jet engines. We know that bridging the gap between these two very different engines required a brilliant leap to traverse the chasm between them, not small incremental steps of the type postulated for Darwinian evolution. Why believe anything different about the origin of eyes? On a different scale, even the simplest organisms have been compared in their complex interdependence with modern aircraft.[5] To change a system in an aircraft generally requires a complex series of adjustments to other systems, otherwise the plane experiences something akin to natural selection—it crashes.[6] Organisms are subject to this limitation.

Interdependence continues beyond organisms, which depend on their physical environment and on each other. A normal healthy human is really an ecological system containing more cells of other organisms than human cells.[7] For example, our intestines contain a diverse flora of bacteria on which we depend for proper bowel function. Outside of ourselves, numerous other organisms participate in great ecological cycles like the nitrogen cycle[8] on which all life depends for existence. Our world operates as an amazingly coordinated system best accounted for by a mind to design its interdependent components and subsystems.

Just as the universe appears from its basic forces up to the structure of the Milky Way and beyond to be built for life to exist on earth, life itself appears designed from the atoms on up to be interdependent. But interdependence is not just about cold, harsh, mechanical necessities; it is also about beauty and wonder. Yes, life involves amazing machinery, but more than that, life is beautiful and it is beautiful to a large degree because of the interdependence that is there. Solomon revealed some of the wisdom God granted him when he recognized this:

> "There are three things that are too amazing for me,
>   four that I do not understand:
> the way of an eagle in the sky,
> the way of a snake on a rock,
> the way of a ship on the high seas,
>   and the way of a man with a maiden."[9]

When it comes to humans, Solomon is most amazed at the way we interact with each other. There is nothing more beautiful in life than the loving interdependence of a man and a woman, on which humanity depends for renewal of our species and provision of sublime joy while alive.

Design and the problem of evil

To the person willing to see design, it is everywhere; the person unwilling to see design grasps at the most reasonable-sounding alternative explanation. Arguments against design commonly assert, "God would not have done it that way." These arguments may invoke imperfection and evil in nature. Even the human genome, with all its wonders has been presented as prone to failure and thus could not have been made by God. John Avise put it this way: "Lesch-Nyhan syndrome[10] hardly seems like the kind of outcome that would be countenanced by a loving all-powerful Diety [*sic*]."[11]

Lesch-Nyhan syndrome is a horrifying disease resulting from gene mutation. Genes make proteins that function in integrated systems. When genes are randomly mutated, the system can be disrupted causing a cascade of effects disrupting other systems and ultimately entire organisms. Nature selects against such changes making natural selection a mechanism of conservation, not of change. The marvel is that organisms are so well-designed that they can withstand amazing disruption and still function on at least a minimal level.

However, belief in a Creator raises profound questions when one looks at the creation and sees the hand of the Creator there. While there is abundant beauty to see, the romantic poet Alfred Lord Tennyson pointed out the tension,

> From scarped cliff and quarried stone
> She [nature] cries, "A thousand types are gone;
> I care for nothing, all shall go." . . .
> Who trusted God was love indeed
> And love Creation's final law
> Tho' Nature, red in tooth and claw
> With ravin, shriek'd against his creed.[12]

If God created all we see, how can He be a good Creator when evil abounds in nature, the cycles of which appear dependent on death and suffering? And what about the overwhelming evidence of death in the fossil record? Options available to a thinking person range from denial of the goodness of God to denial of His involvement, which may ultimately be equivalent to denial of His existence.

Imperfection does not mask design

Even if the design of nature really is evil or fails, an imperfect design does not logically mean something was not designed. The venom delivery system of vipers seems perfectly designed to kill and humans' aching backs look like designs that are prone to failure, but in our experience, brilliantly designed atom bombs and imperfect Ford Pintos have still been the result of design. With bombs and cars, the intentions of the designers can be known to some degree and the success judged accordingly, but with design in nature, can we fully know the intentions of the Designer? Without that knowledge, it is impossible to realistically judge whether a design failed or succeeded.

Absent a good Creator God, what would be the basis for deciding what is evil in nature? Why could not one argue, as Darwin did, that death and struggle are the anvils on which better organisms are forged? What Christians call evil may be the good mechanism of creation! This seems to have been a central element of Nazi ideology. Hitler himself said, "In the limitation of this living space lies the compulsion for the struggle for survival, and the struggle for survival, in turn, contains the precondition for evolution."[13] Absent God as an absolute standard of goodness, what is good becomes relative. Why wouldn't death-driven Darwinism be good?

Alternatively, if imperfect nature testifies to a designer, is the creator evil, as some Gnostics believed? Belief in the goodness of the Creator

-3

requires belief also in a fall—that the creation we now see is not as it came from the hand of the Creator, but is instead a cursed vestige of what once was. Were it not for the willingness of the Creator to subject Himself to the harsh realities of this fallen world, suffering even death to redeem us and the rest of nature,[14] unbelievers might be excused for seeing Christians' belief in the goodness of the Creator God as wishfully blind faith. But even in the fallen creation there is still abundant evidence of its origin from the hand of a beneficent and wise Creator.

Yes, the creation as we now see it is marred in ways that bring suffering to all living things, and yet still there is profound beauty, which is reflected in the way all nature cooperates for the survival of life—the love of mothers for their young, the warm embrace of the person with whom you have decided to spend the rest of your life, and all things that bring true joy. Ultimately, interdependence is about relationships, and all nature tells us that these are both vital for our existence and beautiful to behold. Perhaps the Creator made nature this way to teach us something about the relationship He wishes to have with us, whom He made "in His own image."[15]

This brings us to the very best evidence for a Creator God: He became part of nature and lived among humans. As God and man, Jesus demonstrated His power over nature by raising the dead and ultimately dying, then rising again Himself. This Creator God demonstrates His re-creative power daily in the lives of millions of His "born again" followers who are continually transformed into something new and beautiful. While lesser evidences, like design in the creation, provide a strong case for a Creator, the Creator Himself can be, and wishes to be an intimate part of our daily experience.

Timothy G. Standish *completed his undergraduate education in zoology at Andrews University, Michigan. He commenced his graduate education at the same institution, earning an MS degree in biology while working on brachiopods. George Mason University was the scene of further graduate education where he earned a PhD in environmental biology and public policy while developing molecular techniques for identification and classification of nematode worms. Interactions between science, faith, and public policy are his primary interest. Dr. Standish is an active member of his church and holds a research appointment at the Geoscience Research Institute in Loma Linda, California.*

References

[1] M. T. Cicero, *De Natura Deorum* [On the Nature of the Gods], first century B.C. Available online at http://www.epicurus.net/en/deorum.html.

[2] Romans 1:20, NIV.

[3] For discussion of early ideas about this, see: H. G. Wells, "Another Basis for Life," *Saturday Review* (UK) (December 22, 1894): 676, 677. Reprinted in H. G. Wells, *H. G. Wells: Early Writings in Science and Science Fiction,* introduction by Robert M. Philmus (Berkeley, CA: University of California Press, 1975), 144–147.

[4] The just right nature of the universe is sometimes referred to as the "fine-tuning argument." This is sometimes countered with the "anthropic principle"—we could not exist to observe fine-tuning of the universe unless it is fine-tuned for our existence, so fine-tuning is not necessarily evidence for a designed universe. A useful book on the subject that goes beyond typical arguments is: G. Gonzalez and J. W. Richards, *The Privileged Planet: How Our Place in the Cosmos Is Designed for Discovery* (Washington, DC: Regnery Publishing, Inc., 2004).

[5] "Hoyle on Evolution," *Nature* 294 (1981): 105.

[6] For an example of how a minor engine upgrade on a Boeing 737 led to a crash and death of 47 passengers, see E. J. Trimble, "Report on the Accident to Boeing 737-400 G-OBME Near Kegworth, Leicestershire, on 8 January 1989," HMSO, London (1990). Available online at http://www.aaib.gov.uk/cms_resources.cfm?file=/4-1990%20G-OBME.pdf.

[7] S. R. Gill et al., "Metagenomic Analysis of the Human Distal Gut Microbiome," *Science* 312 (2006): 1355–1359.

[8] H. A. Zuill and T. G. Standish, "Irreducible Interdependence: An IC-like Ecological Property Potentially Illustrated by the Nitrogen Cycle," *Origins* 60 (2007): 6–40.

[9] Proverbs 30:18, 19, NIV.

[10] Lesch-Nyhan syndrome results from mutations in the X-linked gene for hypoxanthine-guanine phosphoribosyltransferase (HGPRT), an enzyme involved in purine metabolism. Symptoms include severe gout, mental retardation, and self-mutilation.

[11] J. Avise, *Inside the Human Genome: A Case for Non-Intelligent Design* (New York: Oxford University Press, U.S.A., 2010), 64.

[12] Alfred Lord Tennyson, *In Memoriam.* These lines are found in canto 56 and appear to be a direct response to *Vestiges of the Natural History of Creation,* published by Robert Chambers in 1844.

[13] A. Hitler, *Zweites Buch* (1928). Krista Smith, trans., *Hitler's Second Book: The Unpublished Sequel to Mein Kampf,* Gerhard L. Weinberg, ed. (New York, NY: Enigma Books, 2004), 2.

[14] See Romans 8:20, 21.

[15] Genesis 1:27, NKJV.

Chapter 6

How Can We Interpret the First Chapters of Genesis?

Some of the most controversial chapters in the Bible are the first eleven chapters of Genesis. Many scientists have argued that everything in the universe, including planet Earth and the life on it, came about by purely natural means—that God had nothing to do with its origins. Most scientists today believe this. In direct contrast, the first eleven chapters of Genesis assert that God, by the mere power of His spoken word, created everything—the sun, moon, stars, this planet, and all life on it.

The key challenge to the Genesis claim comes as a result of the scientific study of nature—what believers refer to as "God's Second Book." As modern scientists have studied the earth—particularly through the disciplines of geology and paleontology—they have observed phenomena in the layers of the earth's crust that they interpret as requiring millions of years to form. In addition, scientists have noticed a sequence of fossils in the geologic column that they suggest shows change or evolution from simple life forms to more complex, modern ones. Finally, as scientists have studied certain radioactive elements in the geologic strata, they have seen that the lowest rocks seem to be very old—some hundreds of millions of years—and that the upper layers gradually show less age. (It should be remembered that most scientists work within a worldview that rejects the idea of God *a priori*—before reaching any conclusion whatsoever—so the explanation for all phenomena encountered are interpreted within a purely naturalistic philosophy.)

Upon putting these observations together—the large number of thick strata, fossil sequences, and radiometric dating—scientists have concluded that the earth and life on it took millions of years to form. This broadly accepted conclusion contradicts the common understanding of the biblical account of origins: God created life on the world by the power of His spoken word in six literal days only a few thousands of years ago.

Influence of modern scientific concepts on biblical scholars

Since the 1800s, many biblical scholars have been strongly influenced by the findings of science in the areas of geology and paleontology as well as by the naturalistic philosophy for understanding the world in a manner that removes God from the picture. These scholars have concluded that the Bible should likewise be viewed through a naturalistic lens. Thus, disregarding Scripture's own description of the revelation/inspiration process, they do not study it as a book of divine origin, but rather consider it a book of purely human origin. Consequently, the Bible is viewed or understood as unreliable since humans are clearly capable of making mistakes. For these scholars, the fact that the Bible was composed in antiquity—before the advent of modern science—makes it even more likely that the Bible's description of origins is erroneous. In view of this critical understanding of the Bible, biblical historical critics proposed an alternate process by which the Bible came into existence. This alternate process denied the Bible's self-claim of supernatural origin, replacing it with the view that text was the outcome of a purely natural, human process.

In the case of Genesis, scholars suggested that the book was not written by Moses under inspiration sometime before 1450 B.C. Rather, Genesis was written and edited by a number of unnamed authors (often referred to as J, E, and P) and "redactors" over a period of several centuries—between 1100 and 450 B.C. Scholars who promote this view—often referred to as "historical critics"—have offered several lines of evidence for their reconstructions of Genesis. They point to phenomena in the Genesis text such as apparent doublets, contradictions, and anachronisms in an attempt to show the complex, diachronic manner in which Genesis was composed. The identification of these purported phenomena in the text have led them to suggest, for example, that Genesis 1 and 2 present contradictory creation accounts written at different times and for different purposes.

Their rejection of the supernatural manifested in the world has also led these critics to reject any supernatural or miraculous claims in the Bible, such as the idea that God could create the earth and its life forms merely by speaking, and that this occurred over the course of only six days. The critics prefer to accept the conclusions reached by the bulk of contemporary science—that the earth and its life forms came into existence through purely natural processes over millions of years. Also rejected is the idea that the entire surface of the earth as we know it was destroyed by a divinely initiated flood. For them, no global flood occurred. And if there was any flood at all, it was only local in nature.

The biblical critics also argue that the Creation account in Genesis is full of naïve ideas that prove the account cannot be historically true or scientifically plausible. For example, they claim the Hebrews possessed a naïve cosmology—an unscientific understanding of the structure of the universe. Pulling together different biblical texts, and making some assumptions about what neighboring ancient Near Eastern peoples thought, the biblical critics reconstructed what they thought the Hebrews would have actually believed about the nature of the universe. In this reconstructed Hebrew cosmos, the heavens were seen to be like a hollow upside-down metal bowl resting over a flat earth, with the sun, moon, and stars fixed to the underside of the dome where they could be seen by humans at night. The dome was also thought to have gates allowing for the occasional flow of water (rain) from the waters above the heavens. The critics also assumed the ancient Hebrews believed in large subterranean seas and a literal hell.

Responding to critical arguments

Each of the arguments put forth by the historical critics for the non-inspired, alternate origin of Genesis has been thoroughly critiqued by biblical scholars who reject the historical critical method. For example, careful analysis of the word for "day" (*yom*) in the Creation account shows it does not mean an indefinite period of time, but rather, a literal day of about twenty-four hours such as we know today.[1] Thus, the Bible does indeed state that God created the world in six days, and rested on the seventh. Similarly, an analysis of the Hebrew word for flood (*mabbul*) shows it to be a unique word for a global water catastrophe leading to the literal destruction of the entire world—a "de-creation" of the work God had executed during Creation week.[2] As for the idea that the Hebrews had a naïve view of the cosmos, recent studies of the Hebrew word for firmament (*raqia*) show it does not mean an upside-down metal bowl.[3] Indeed, a review of the history of critical biblical scholarship shows that nineteenth-century scholars were the inventors of the belief that the ancient peoples (Hebrews and others) conceived of a flat earth with a metallic half-domed sky.[4]

Other challenges concerning the unity and antiquity of the Creation/Flood account have also been addressed. For example, the presence of doublets (e.g., two different names for God [*elohim* and *Yahweh*][5] and the telling of the Creation story twice in Genesis 1 and 2) has been shown to be a common narrative technique in ancient Near Eastern literature, and thus does not necessarily reflect the existence of more than one author.[6]

Apparent contradictions—such whether plants were created on day 4 of Creation week (Genesis 1) or were not added until after the Creation week was finished (Genesis 2)—have been convincingly explained. In the example mentioned, the Hebrew words for plants in chapter 1 are different from those used in chapter 2.[7] The plants created on day 4 in chapter 1 are those of fruit trees suitable for food. In contrast, the plants found in chapter 2 include thorns and thistles or certain grasslike plants requiring considerable work to bring to harvest. The context of chapter 2 clearly shows these second group of plants came about as the result of sin.

Finally, the appearance of the so-called anachronisms in Genesis—for example, the appearance of tents and camels in the second millennium B.C.—has been shown, in many cases, not to be anachronisms at all. Renowned Egyptologist and scholar, Dr. Kenneth Kitchen, has shown that tents were common in the ancient Near East in the second millennium—just as the Bible describes.[8] Similarly, the presence of camels prior to the time of David has also been well-documented in recent times.[9] I had the privilege of contributing to this conclusion upon discovering an ancient petroglyph (rock carving) of a man leading a camel by a rope in a Bronze Age context (pre-1400 B.C.) north of the traditional location of Mount Sinai (Wadi Nasib).

Significant literary features of Genesis

A number of literary features in Genesis, such as the structure of Genesis 1–11, are more typical of the second millennium before the Christian era than the first—suggesting that much of Genesis reflects earlier times. For example, several second millennium "primeval histories" exist—origin stories such as the Akkadian "Atrahasis Epic" and the Sumerian "Eridu Genesis" with which Genesis 1–11 has much in common. Among these feature is a clear organization by parts—all three of these primeval history stories contain three sections—a creation story, the rise of a problem, and a judgment by flood.

While ancient Mesopotamian cultures produced later flood stories (like the Gilgamesh Epic) and creation stories (like the Enuma Elish), these later versions were no longer "complete" primeval histories containing all three elements—creation, problem, flood.[10] The fact that all three exist in Genesis would indicate that Genesis was composed at the same time as its Mesopotamian counterparts—in the second millennium. That fits with the biblical view that Moses wrote the book of Genesis sometime before 1400 B.C. Of course, the Genesis version is significantly different from its Mesopotamian counterparts. In fact, several scholars have noted that the author of Genesis was deliberately challenging the Mesopotamian version by being "polemical."[11] That is, the author of Genesis was disagreeing with the Mesopotamian version of creation and was claiming to provide the correct version of how things came into being.

It is worth noting that a number of literary features in Genesis 1–11 suggest the author intended to provide a historical narrative of earth's early history—not simply a theological statement, or a nonliteral, literary depiction of Creation such as a poem, parable, saga, myth, etc. For example, a unity of the narrative of Genesis 1–11 continues into the rest of Genesis and, indeed, runs into the book of Exodus. Together, these books tell a continuous story from Creation, through Abraham, Joseph, the descent down to Egypt, and the Exodus. In fact, the Creation story of Genesis 1–11 has been identified by many scholars as a prologue to the rest of the Pentateuch. Second, a certain Hebrew verbal form exists—the waw-consecutive—that is typically used for historical narratives (such as is found in books like the Chronicles and Kings). The waw-consecutive is found in the Creation account as well, suggesting historical intent and purpose for the narrative. A third literary feature clearly points to the "historical impulse" of these chapters: The appearance of *toledoth* formulae, usually translated as "these are the generations of. . . ." Finally, many elements in Ancient Near East parallels of primeval histories can be shown to be historical.[12]

Summary

Taken together, this evidence suggests that it remains eminently reasonable to conclude that (1) Genesis is in fact an early literary work—the product of the second millennium before the Christian era;

(2) the text was composed as a unified account, although there may have been some minor editorial work at a later time; and (3) the text was intended to be understood by its authors as an authentic account of earth's origins in which the world was created in six days and later destroyed by a global flood.

Randall W. Younker holds BA and MA degrees in religion and biology from Pacific Union College and an MA and a PhD in Near Eastern archaeology from the University of Arizona. He serves as professor of Old Testament and Biblical Archaeology at the Seventh-day Adventist Seminary of Andrews University, where he is also the director of the Institute of Archaeology and the Siegfried Horn Museum. Dr. Younker has directed numerous interdisciplinary seasons of archaeological field research in Israel and Jordan and is a trustee of the American Schools of Oriental Research. He has co-edited seven books, and published scores of scholarly articles.

References

[1] See Gerhard F. Hasel, "The 'Days' of Creation in Genesis 1: Literal 'Days' or Figurative 'Periods/Epochs' of Time?" *Origins* 21, no. 1 (1994): 5–38. Hasel shows that the Hebrew clearly means literal days in Genesis 1.

[2] See Kenneth A. Mathews, *The New American Commentary: Genesis 1–11:26* (Nashville: Broadman and Holman Publishers, 1996), 365, 366, where he argues that the author is using *mabbul* to refer to a cataclysm that was worldwide in scope.

[3] See Robert C. Newman, *The Biblical Firmament: Vault or Vapor?* (Hatfield, PA: Interdisciplinary Biblical Research Institute, 2000). Newman's position is supported by commentators such as Mathews (150).

[4] Jeffrey Burton Russell, *Inventing the Flat Earth* (Westport, CT: Praeger, 1991). For an exhaustive discussion about what the ancients since the time of Christ thought about the heavens, see Edward Grant, *Planets, Stars, and Orbs: The Medieval Cosmos, 1200–1687* (Cambridge: Cambridge University Press, 1994).

[5] See Kenneth A. Kitchen, *Ancient Orient and Old Testament* (Downers Grove, IL: InterVarsity Press, 1966), 121–123, where he provides numerous examples from Egypt and Mesopotamia.

[6] See Isaac M. Kikawada, "The Double Creation of Mankind in Enki and Ninmah, Atrahasis I 1–351, and Genesis 1–2," *Iraq* 45 (1983): 43–45; and Duane Garrett, *Rethinking Genesis: The Sources and Authorship of the First Book of the Pentateuch* (Grand Rapids, MI: Baker, 1991), 21–25.

[7] See Umberto Cassuto, *A Commentary on the Book of* Genesis (Jerusalem: Magnes Press, 1964), especially his discussion of plants in Genesis 1 and 2.

[8] Kenneth A. Kitchen, *The Bible in Its World: The Bible and Archaeology Today* (Downers Grove, IL: InterVarsity Press, 1977), 58, 59. See also James Hoffmeier, "Tents in Egypt and the Ancient Near East," *JSSEA* 7, no. 3 (1977): 13–28, and Robert C. Newman (2000).

[9] Kenneth A. Kitchen, *On the Reliability of the Old Testament* (Grand Rapids, MI: Eerdmans, 2003), 338, 339.

[10] See Kenneth A. Kitchen (1977), 31–36, and Kitchen (2003), 422–427 for a more extensive discussion.

[11] G. F. Hasel, "The Polemic Nature of the Genesis Cosmology," *Evangelical Quarterly* 46 (1974): 81–102.

[12] For a discussion of the historicity of the Genesis narratives, see Raymond B. Dillard and Tremper Longman III, *An Introduction to the Old Testament* (Grand Rapids, MI: Zondervan, 1994), 49, 50; again, see Kitchen (2003), 422–427, who discusses the historical aspects of the early Genesis accounts in their ancient Near Eastern literary contexts.

Chapter 7

What Are the Meaning and Implications of the Big Bang Theory?

"If I understand you correctly," said the student after the Professor had explained the Big Bang theory of the Universe, "first there was nothing and then it exploded."[1]

A few centuries ago, natural scientists saw in their object of study the working of a powerful, sovereign God, whose action could be invoked when science was unable to provide answers. Since advances in science provided answers to many of the formerly unanswered questions without invoking God, scientists began to believe they would ultimately be able to answer all questions through the correct application of purely naturalistic methods and reasoning. The Big Bang theory of the origin, development, and structure of our Universe[2] is the result of science's efforts towards this goal.

All scientific disciplines focusing on nature, the earth, and life are based on the study of matter in all its forms. The Big Bang theory claims to provide an explanation for the origin of all matter that is studied in

78

these disciplines. As a result, Big Bang cosmology has become an all-embracing envelope, providing a framework not only for the study of the physical Universe but also for all natural science disciplines. However, the Big Bang is more than a cosmology; it is also a philosophy based on a naturalistic worldview.[3]

The theory and its problems

The Big Bang theory about the origin and subsequent development of the Universe had its origins in the 1920s and '30s when the American astronomer Edwin Hubble discovered the so-called "red-shift"—the phenomenon of a shift toward the red end of the spectrum by light coming from distant galaxies.[4] Hubble interpreted this as evidence that all distant galaxies are moving away from earth. The simplest interpretation is that the early Universe must have once been much smaller, and is now expanding at high speed. This interpretation of the red-shift is one of the strongest pillars of the Big Bang theory. Other interpretations are possible, though somewhat speculative.

The Cosmic Microwave Background Radiation (CMBR) is another pillar of the Big Bang theory. CMBR refers to the faint microwave radiation that fills the Universe, virtually to the same extent in all directions. This radiation is considered to have been emitted some 370,000 years after the Big Bang, when radiation de-coupled from matter. Galaxies in the Local Group (of which our Milky Way is a member) are moving at a velocity of 600 km/s with respect to the CMBR. This fact is at odds with the CMBR's observed isotropy[5] (i.e., that the radiation has the same value when measured in different directions). This could be caused by a superstrong gravitational "attractor" that has not yet been satisfactorily identified.

The theory's third pillar lies in the abundances of the chemical elements, especially the ratio of hydrogen to helium (H/He), which accords very well with theoretical calculations. However, these calculations depend on parameters such as the ratio of photons to baryons (i.e., units of light energy to units of matter, such as atoms). Because these parameters cannot be measured accurately, they enter into the equations as free parameters, which are variables that are used in order to define a theory well enough to make a prediction. Our inability to verify the values of these variables by observation means they are subject to a high degree of uncertainty.

Perplexing problems

In the last thirty years a number of other perplexing problems with the Big Bang theory have come to light. The isotropy of the CMBR implies that matter and energy are very evenly distributed in the Universe. This makes it difficult to explain how galaxies can form—whether by the grouping of stars or whether stars form inside existing galaxies.

A second difficulty is the "horizon" problem. The CMBR's isotropy suggests that widely separated parts of the Universe have the same temperature and energy density, although they are too far apart for radiation from these parts to have reached each other within the lifetime of the Universe.

Third is the "flatness" problem, which deals with the exceptionally fine-tuning of the Universe's mass density. A slightly imperfect fine-tuning would signify that the Universe would have either collapsed long ago (if the density of matter were too high) or dispersed too rapidly for stars to form (if the density of matter were too low). Fine-tuning requiring a precision of about 1 to 10^{55} is being quoted[6] and raises the question of how to explain this extraordinary coincidence, which is precisely the necessary one for human life to exist.

To solve these problems, Alan Guth proposed the concept of "inflation."[7] At the extremely high temperatures of the very early Universe, gravity would have been a repulsive force making the Universe expand for a fraction of a second at speeds much greater than the speed of light. Inflation solves the problem of galaxy formation, the horizon problem, and the flatness problem.

Problems remain, however. The most important and annoying of these is that inflation predicts an energy density that is exactly at the critical level between eternal expansion and premature collapse. This expansion of the Universe is governed by its mass density. Observations show that the amount of detectable matter in the Universe is less than 10 percent of the amount required for a "flat" universe.[8] This is the problem of the missing or "dark" matter. The favored answer to this question is that most of the mass of the Universe consists of exotic "dark matter" that does not consist of protons and neutrons (nonbaryonic matter). Ideas abound regarding the nature of this matter, but none seem to provide a satisfactory answer.

Gravity will slow down the expansion of the Universe, but observations show that at a large distance it is slowing down less than expected. The implied force reducing the slowing down is described by the cosmological constant, Λ (lambda), and is equivalent to a uniform energy density that exerts a repulsive force. Particle physics has no explanation for Λ, but calculations have been made of the strength of the inferred force needed to explain this so-called vacuum energy density thought to be present in the Universe. These calculations indicate that the repulsive force should be about 10^{120} times larger than the observed effect on the rate of slowing down. This enormous disparity between the calculations of the force required and the observed effect led Nobel laureate Steven Weinberg to quip, "This must be the worst failure of an order-of-magnitude estimate in the history of science."[9]

Besides its scientific problems, the Big Bang theory also poses problems of a philosophical nature. Like all physical theories, the Big Bang theory rests on a number of assumptions one must make in order to have an explanatory framework for one's observations. The Cosmological Principle (CP) states that, on a sufficiently large scale, all observers, wherever located in the Universe, see the same features that we see. The CP has been postulated to provide the required explanatory framework. It includes the thesis that the laws of physics as we know them from our terrestrial studies are likewise valid at every location in the Universe. While this assumption must be made to be able to do any extraterrestrial physics, there is no logical reason why it should be true.

Remarkable coincidences

Besides the apparent fine-tuning required to solve the flatness problem, there are another hundred instances where physical quantities and other conditions of nature are found to be precisely fine-tuned so that life as we know it can exist.[10] This can be seen as a strong indicator of the existence of an intelligent designer interested in populating earth with human beings.

In addition, the location of earth in the Universe is such that it provides the best possible platform for discovering the Universe's characteristics[11]—in other words, to do cosmology. Bible passages such as Psalm 19:1 ("The heavens declare the glory of God; the skies proclaim the work of his hands," NIV) and Isaiah 40:26 ("Lift up your eyes and look to the heavens: Who created all these? He who brings out the starry host one by one, and calls them each by name. Because of his great power and mighty strength, not one of them is missing," NIV) lead Christians to think of God as the Creator who shows Himself through His handiwork so that we may know and love Him. And, of course, the beginning of space, time, and everything that the Big Bang points to cannot fail to bring Genesis 1:1 to mind. Note, however, that "In the beginning" does not give us precise chronological information other than to point to a period of time prior to Creation Week some six thousand years ago.[12]

Implications

The Universe's isotropy could be considered evidence that earth is at or very near the center of a spherically symmetric Universe. Since this idea might point in the direction of a God who has a special purpose for His creatures,[13] it is scientific anathema. The Cosmological Principle (CP) avoids this conclusion and places earth in a general, random location in the Universe. However, there are theoretical arguments why the CP may not be valid in the as-yet unobserved outer reaches of the Universe.[14] If observations should prove this to be true, then cosmology of the remote Universe would cease to be a science and—perish the thought—degenerate into speculation. For the Christian this may not be a problem if, for example, God has seen fit to isolate our part of the Universe from the rest of creation because of the presence of sin.

Claus Eisbart makes this perceptive statement: "Ultimately, science consists of human activities, and we may describe these activities as scientific because of their aims and the way the aims are pursued, without having to say that the aims are in fact realized or can be realized. In this sense, cosmology clearly constitutes a science. But it would not make sense to regard cosmology as a science if it tries to pursue aims that can obviously not be fulfilled."[15]

A good example of this situation is the introduction of the idea of a "multiverse"—the supposed existence of a very large collection of different universes each with their own characteristics. If these characteristics were the results of random circumstances, it would not be impossible for our universe to be just right for life. This is one form of the Anthropic Principle,[16] which says in general that the properties of the Universe must be such that life can exist in it. If it were not so, we would not be here to talk about it!

As I write this, there is considerable discussion in Adventist circles about the order and time frame of God's creative acts. One scenario especially popular among evangelical Christians is that of Theistic Evolution: God directed evolution's progress from simple to complex, and bridges difficulties like the origins of matter and of life. Edward Zinke has given a clear theological exposition of how theistic evolution paints a picture of God at odds with the biblical description of His attributes.[17]

Richard Davidson[18] provides a short and to-the-point discussion where, among other scenarios, he summarizes the traditional view—i.e., the initial unformed, unfilled state of the earth—as follows: (1) God is before all creation; (2) there is an absolute beginning of time with regard to this world and its surrounding heavenly spheres; (3) God creates the heavens and earth but they are at first "unformed" and "unfilled"; (4)

on the first day of the seven-day Creation week, God begins to form and fill; (5) God accomplishes His work in six successive literal twenty-four-hour days; and (6) God rests on the seventh day, blessing and sanctifying it as a memorial of Creation.

Conclusion

Naturalistic science works within a paradigm, simply stated as, "All there ever was, is, and will be, are mass, time, energy, and motion." This paradigm is embedded in a naturalistic worldview where any role for God has been excluded from the start. As a result, attempts to understand the obviously nonmaterial aspects of life on this planet—love and hate, joy and sadness, conscience, beauty, etc.—in purely scientific terms are doomed to failure. Neither are deeper questions of life addressed. This has not stopped natural scientists trying to understand them in purely naturalistic terms,[19] but these explanations—if that is what we should call them at all—are often contrived, devoid of proper and valid fundamental principles and, therefore, unacceptable.

Philosopher Bertrand Russell stated, "What science cannot tell us, mankind cannot know."[20] I am glad that God tells us about many aspects of the Universe that lie outside naturalistic science. Leading cosmologist George Ellis wrote, "We are unable to obtain a model of the universe without some specifically cosmological assumptions which are completely unverifiable."[21] Awesome confession!

Mart de Groot studied astronomy at the University of Utrecht, the Netherlands, obtaining a doctorate degree in 1969. He worked at the European Southern Observatory in Chile (1970–1976) and was director of (1976–1994) and senior research associate (1994–2000) at the Armagh Observatory in Northern Ireland. He holds an honorary ScD from Andrews University, Michigan, and entered the ministry in 1997. Presently semi-retired, he pastors a Seventh-day Adventist church in Northern Ireland. He published many astronomical research articles, edited a few books, wrote several articles for church magazines, and speaks regularly on matters concerning science and faith.

References

[1] Johan van Os, *Reader's Digest,* February 1992, 92.

[2] I use "Universe" (with capital *U*) to mean the physical, extraterrestrial universe.

[3] See chapter 1 in this book for more on worldviews.

[4] The distance to a galaxy is estimated by the amount of shifting of the light.

[5] M. S. Turner and A. Tyson, "Cosmology at the Millennium," *Reviews of Modern Physics* 71 (1999): S145; T. R. Lauer and M. Postman, "The Motion of the Local Group," *Astrophysical Journal* 425 (1994): 418.

[6] J. V. Narlikar, "Did the Universe Originate in a Big Bang?" in *Cosmic Perspectives,* S. K. Biswas, ed. (Cambridge: University Press, 1989).

[7] Alan Guth, *The Inflationary Universe: The Quest for a New Theory of Cosmic Origins* (New York: Perseus, 1997).

[8] Peter Coles, "The End of the Model Universe," *Nature* 393 (1998): 741.

[9] S. Weinberg, *Dreams of a Final Theory* (New York: Pantheon, 1992).

[10] Hugh Ross, *The Creator and the Cosmos* (Colorado Springs, CO: NavPress, 2001).

[11] G. Gonzales and J. W. Richards, *The Privileged Planet* (Washington, DC: Regnery Publ. Co., 2004).

[12] R. M. Davidson, "In the Beginning: How to Interpret Genesis 1," *Dialogue* 6, no. 3 (1994): 9.

[13] Ellen G. White, *The Great Controversy* (Mountain View, CA: Pacific Press®, 1950), 677.

[14] Claus Eisbart, "Can We Justifiably Assume the Cosmological Principle in Order to Break Model Underdetermination in Cosmology?" *Journal for General Philosophy of Science* 40, no. 2 (2009): 175.

[15] Ibid.

[16] J. D. Barrow and F. J. Tipler, *The Anthropic Cosmological Principle* (London: Oxford University Press, 1988).

[17] E. Edward Zinke, "Theistic Evolution: Implications for the Role of Creation in Seventh-day Adventist Theology," in *Creation, Catastrophe, and Calvary,* John T. Baldwin, ed. (Hagerstown, MD: Review and Herald, 2000), 159.

[18] R. M. Davidson, "In the Beginning," 9.

[19] Richard Dawkins, *The God Delusion* (London: Black Swan, 2006).

[20] B. Russell, *Religion and Science* (London: Oxford University Press, 1961), 235; see also http://cantseetheforest.org/2006/09/28/quotations-from-bertrand-russell/.

[21] G. F. R. Ellis, "Cosmology and Verifiability," *Quarterly Journal of the Royal Astronomical Society* 16 (1975): 245, 246.

Chapter 8

When Did Creation Occur?

Some conservative Christians insist that the earth is only some 6,000 years old. The scientific community insists that vertebrates go back some 500 million years, and that the earth itself goes back some 4.6 billion years. Who, if anyone, is right, and does it really matter? In this chapter we will make some background observations, then consider different models for creation and the biblical, theological, and scientific evidence relevant to those models. We will then consider the implications of our choice of model for when creation took place.

Preliminary considerations

Before we discuss the above question, we should answer a preliminary question: "Did creation take place?" I am going to assume the answer is Yes. Nature did not create itself. Reasons for that answer can be found in *Signature in the Cell* by Steve Meyer,[1] as well as in *The Edge of Evolution* by Michael Behe,[2] and *Science Discovers God* by Ariel Roth,[3] and for that matter in *The Privileged Planet* by Guillermo Gonzalez and

Jay Richards.[4] See also the chapter by Timothy Standish in this volume.[5] If we accept the concept that God did indeed create the universe and life, and that the results of this creation are detectable, several important consequences follow:

1. Atheism is not a valid option for our worldview.
2. The scientific consensus cannot be trusted implicitly, particularly where there are theological consequences. The consensus has been wrong on intelligent design, and it is reasonable to ask if it could be wrong elsewhere.
3. We must review the actual data if we want to arrive at the truth.
4. Attempting to explain natural history in its entirety without regard to the supernatural element is an invalid exercise.
5. Reliable eyewitness accounts are more important in determining history than is scientific reasoning.
6. Theological reasoning becomes as important for determining historical facts as scientific reasoning (and it becomes indispensable to have the right theology).

That last consequence may be surprising to many, but if we take a moment to think about it, predicting what God would do in a given situation depends more on theology than on science.

Possible options

With this background, we are now ready to consider the question, "When did creation take place?" It might help to consider several answers. For the moment, we will not consider the creation of the universe, or even the solar system. The most important theological question here is, "When did the creation of life take place?" Some proposed answers are:

A. Life was the result of front-loading of the universe with very precise initial conditions, or physically instantiated information, so that without any physical laws being broken, life developed about 3.8 billion years ago and continued to develop according to plan. Creation may be thought of as being completed at the Big Bang (or whenever the universe originated), but the results were not seen until a few billion years ago.

B. God specifically intervened at the origin of life some 3.8 billion years ago, and then possibly again several times, including at the Cambrian explosion. In between God's interventions, nature followed the usual laws.

C. God has continually guided a process of gradually increasing complexity, with life starting some 3.8 billion years ago, with overt miracles being rare, but covert ones being common. Evolution is in reality a guided process, contrary to what is stated in most textbooks.

D. Life started some 3.8 billion years ago, but the intervention that has produced increasingly complex forms came from demonic sources rather than from God. God then stepped in a few thousand years ago and created Adam and Eve, who then fell, and the rest of history is reflected in the biblical record.

E. God created all life in the short period of time described by Genesis, and what we see in the fossil record is the result of a recent flood rather than millions to billions of years claimed in standard geological theory.[6]

It is difficult to test the differences between theories A, B, and C, and their theological consequences are also difficult to distinguish, and so for our purposes they will be lumped together. We thus have three options for the creation of life: old divine creation, old demonic creation, and recent creation. We will consider three lines of evidence: biblical, theological, and scientific.

Biblical considerations

We will now consider the biblical evidence. If one reads the story in Genesis 1, it is clear that the story reads like history,[7] with the days being ordinary days consisting of an evening and a morning.[8] In the era before the rise of modern geology, the story was interpreted, with rare exceptions, as describing six ordinary days.[9]

The significant Christian exceptions are Origen and Augustine. Origen was famous for allegorical interpretations of the Bible. Augustine[10] is particularly interesting in that his arguments for an instantaneous creation, rather than one in six days, are three. The biblical argument was based on Ecclesiasticus (or Sirach) 18:1, which reads, "He that liveth for ever / Hath created all things in general." In Augustine's Latin Bible, the last word read *simul,* meaning instantaneously. This was a poor translation of the original Greek, which read *koine,* well-translated by the King James Version "in general" quoted above. Augustine's philosophical argument was that a creation that took time would not be perfect, as it implied intermediate imperfect steps, and that this would be unworthy of a perfect God. Augustine's scientific argument was that it made no sense for light to travel around the world before the sun was created.

Those arguments do not work today. The biblical argument on the basis of a poor translation of an apocryphal verse doesn't hold water. The philosophical necessity of an instantaneously perfect creation is by no means obvious. And light no longer has to travel around the earth for the first three days—all it has to do is be unidirectional. The earth turns. (It is also interesting to note that Augustine made his mistake in interpretation on the basis of philosophy and the science of the day. This might be a cautionary tale for our time.)

Thus, if the biblical account has any weight, it supports a six-day creation that occurred in the recent past.

Theological considerations

Theologically, there appears to be no advantage to the idea that God took a long time to create life on earth. But there do exist two theological considerations that favor the recent creation of life over old divine creation, one of which appears to favor recent creation over old demonic creation as well. In addition, old demonic creation has its own theological difficulties.

The first theological consideration is that of death before sin. Romans 5 clearly states that through one man's sin, death passed upon all, for all have sinned, and that the wages of sin is death. The difficulty with old divine creation is that if one accepts the standard geological interpretation of the fossil record, death, including predation and disease, occurred before any reasonable interpretation of the time of Adam. According to this model death of hominids occurred before Adam. One can claim that they were not truly human, but the biblical writers seem concerned about nature as well as about humankind. Romans 8:19–23 indicates that not just humankind, but that creation itself was involved in the Fall and that it will be redeemed along with us. Matthew 10:29–31 indicates that God pays attention to the death of sparrows. Isaiah 11 and Isaiah 65 seem to indicate that animal death will not be part of the new earth, raising the question of whether it was part of God's original creation.

Demonic old creation does not share this problem to the same degree. Demonic old creation can blame pre-Adamic death on a sinner, namely Satan. Thus, human death could be the result of Adam's sin, and animal death could be the result of Satan's sin. Death before sin is a problem mainly to old divine creation.

The second problem is that of natural evil, such things as earthquakes, floods, and tornadoes. The problem of human-caused evil is usually solved by postulating that God gave us free will, and that since it is truly free, God is not responsible for our choices—we are. The risk of allowing people to choose wrongly is usually felt to be outweighed by the benefit of the possibility of true love, which requires freedom. But if we accept that defense, it only justifies God in the case of human-caused evil. That defense does not justify Him in the case of natural evil. Death by volcanic eruption, tsunami, or flood does not seem to be as easy to explain on the basis of human decision, at least given an old divine creation model. And here, even an old demonic creation model might have trouble.

But a recent creation model can escape this criticism. For in this model, after the third day of creation (when the dry land appeared), major tectonic plate movement probably was absent until the Flood (or at least until the Fall), implying no death caused by volcanoes, major earthquakes, or tsunamis. With a fairly uniform, mild, rainless climate, hurricanes, tornadoes, and floods would be nonexistent, as presumably would be droughts. And finally, such diseases as cancer would be absent according to Revelation 22:2. So most, if not all, natural evil would also be the result of human sin, thus releasing God from direct responsibility for this evil also.

Old demonic creation partially avoids these problems. But it has its own theological problems, for it comes very close to duplicating the old Gnostic idea that a lesser god created the material universe, or at least the living creatures in our part of it. There is also the problem of the relationship of the demonic creation to the divine creation. Did God re-create everything, including ginkgo trees, coelecanths, and horseshoe crabs, that are found in the fossil record and also today? In that case, why did He use the devil's models? Or are all animals that can be dated over, say, fifty thousand years ago actually demonic creations, and not "very good" as Genesis 1 seems to imply? Perhaps more to the point, did some hominids survive after Adam, and some humans have more or less demon-created blood in them? Or did all the hominids besides humans get killed off? In that case, why do we look so much like previous hominids? This is not to say that some solution cannot be found. But it does suggest that there is some strain in the theory, which is at present not relieved. The problem, of course, does not exist with either old divine creation or recent creation.

So, given the above options, theological considerations seem to be supportive of a recent creation.

Scientific considerations

We finally come to the strongest argument for an old creation, that there is "overwhelming evidence" from science for long ages. But we need to be careful here. We have already seen a theologically charged area where the scientific consensus has turned out to be wrong: intelligent design theory. In recent years, the scientific consensus has been protected by occurrences such as the official retracting of a peer-reviewed paper,[11] the denial of employment and tenure for supporters of intelligent design, and the removal of teaching responsibilities from an individual holding tenure who was a recognized world authority in his field.[12] A philosophically/theologically motivated resistance against the Big Bang theory has also been initiated by atheists. Thus, if short-age creationists are suppressed when their beliefs become public,[13] it is reasonable to suspect that the "settled consensus" on the age of life on earth may also be driven by philosophical and sociological considerations.

In addition, we must note that there are some contrary data that are rarely mentioned in the mainstream science journals, and especially in the textbooks. Some examples are listed below.

Erosion rates are too rapid. Erosion rates, even under uniformitarian conditions, are fast enough to cause severe problems for the current standard geologic timescale. One can compensate for that with uplift, but this leaves unexplained the existence of Phanerozoic rock on the top of such places as Mount Everest and the Alps.[14]

Sedimentary gaps. There is the widespread existence of gaps of millions of years in the fossil record, without evidence of the expected erosion between the layers.[15]

Evidence of soft sediments. Polystrate fossils, extending through several bedding planes, indicate rapid burial activity.[16] Soft sediment deformation, and various intrusions of layers of sediment into each other,[17] show that both (or all) sedimentary layers were soft at the same time.

Amino acid racemization. Amino acids in living organisms are in a chemical form, known as the L-form. Over time, L-amino acids tend to change to a mixture of L- and R-forms, at a rate that is thought to be constant. Comparison of rates calculated from fossil material shows a progressive decrease in amino acid racemization constants with time, which is essentially removed if a short timescale is assumed.[18]

Fresh biological material. There are viable bacteria supposedly millions of years old,[19] and tissue in dinosaurs that was not expected based on their supposed age.[20]

Genetic deterioration. There is the question of how species can persist for millions of years with the present mutation rate, suggesting that a short timescale is mandated by the mere fact that life is present today.[21]

Anomalous radioisotope dates. Even in the field of radiometric dating, there is evidence from carbon-14 dating,[22] beryllium-10 dating,[23] and uranium-lead dating[24] that argues that the current timescale may be incorrect.

Radiometric dating is most often cited as "proving" a long timescale. But there are two possible explanations of radiometric dating that are consistent with a short timescale. First, in some cases the "clock" can be documented not to be reset to zero during geological events, such as melting, that have usually been assumed to have reset it. Argon can be retained, and isochron lines can be mimicked by mixing lines.[25] Second, there is strongly suggestive evidence that accelerated radioactive decay has occurred in the past, and this may precisely mimic old age in most dating systems.[26] There is even some reason to believe that both explanations are important.[27]

Conclusion

The above considerations are not intended to be exhaustive, or to imply that more work is not needed on the recent creation model. However, they should suggest that such a model provides a good explanation for a considerable amount of scientific evidence that cannot be explained well by competing models. Given the strong biblical and theological support for a recent creation model, it seems reasonable to give this model serious consideration, and in my opinion it should be the favored model.

But isn't short-age creationism falsified by multiple lines of evidence? The question betrays a profound misunderstanding of how science works. Science is not in the business of falsifying theories. That earlier Popperian concept has itself been shown to be inaccurate. What might naïvely be thought of as falsification turns out to be viewed from inside a theoretical framework as anomalies. Although anomalies do not help a theory, they rarely cause its overthrow. The theory is rather abandoned when it fails to produce new results, or novel facts, as they are known in the philosophy of science.

Short-age creationism has produced just such novel facts. Supracontinental paleocurrents and carbon-14 in fossil carbon were suspected from a short-age perspective and not from any long-age perspective. They were, in fact, discovered by short-age creationists. Some of the other scientific findings listed above, although discovered by adherents to long age, were not known until after short-age theory was well-developed, and would still qualify as novel facts. When one runs into an apparent falsification, it is appropriate to ask if that falsification will disappear after further research is done. Creationists need not quit when faced with a difficult problem.

Paul A. L. Giem *received a BA in religion with a major in chemistry from Union College, and an MA in religion and an MD from Loma Linda University. He has published original research in religion and in medicine, and also has done original research in carbon-14 dating. He is currently board certified in emergency medicine and internal medicine, and works as an emergentologist, urgent care physician, and hospitalist in the southern California area. His publications include the book* Scientific Theology *(1997), available at http://www.scientifictheology.com.*

References

[1] New York: Harper Collins Publishers, 2009.

[2] New York: Free Press, 2007.

[3] Hagerstown, MD: Review and Herald, 2008.

[4] Washington, DC: Regnery Publishing, Inc., 2004.

[5] Intelligent design theory does not prove the existence of God, but is widely recognized as being religion-friendly.

[6] The question of exactly how many thousands of years ago creation occurred will not be dealt with here. The Masoretic text suggests around six thousand, the Septuagint seventy-five hundred, and various other ages have been suggested. But there is no theory that postulates a creation of complex life between about one hundred thousand years and five hundred million years. This difference can serve to distinguish between short-age and long-age theories.

[7] For example, it uses the standard narrative form, the waw-consecutive. See Steven W. Boyd, "Statistical Determination of Genre in Biblical Hebrew: Evidence for a Historical Reading of Genesis 1:1–2:3," in *Radioisotopes and the Age of the Earth: Results of a Young-Earth Creationist Research*

Initiative, Larry Vardiman, Andrew A. Snelling, and Eugene F. Chaffin, eds., vol. 2 (El Cajon, CA: Institute for Creation Research, 2005), 631–734. Available online at http://www.icr.org/article/ statistical-determination-genre-biblical (all Web references accessed September 29, 2010).

[8] See Gerhard F. Hasel, "The 'Days' of Creation in Genesis 1: Literal 'Days' or Figurative 'Periods/ Epochs' of Time?" *Origins* 21 (1994): 5–36. Available online at http://www.grisda.org/origins/21005.pdf .

[9] See Seraphim Rose, *Genesis, Creation, and Early Man: The Orthodox Christian Vision* (Platina, CA: Saint Herman of Alaska Brotherhood, 2000).

[10] *De Genesi ad Litteram.* There are now a couple of English translations, one by Taylor and one by Quasten et al.

[11] The paper was S. C. Meyer, "The Origin of Biological Information and the Higher Taxonomic Categories," *Proceedings Biological Society of Washington* 117, no. 2 (2004): 213–239. Available online at http://www.discovery.org/a/2177. The official reasons for withdrawal, according to the Statement From the Council of the Biological Society of Washington (available at: web.archive.org/web /20070926214521/http://www.biolsocwash.org/id_statement.html), were that "contrary to typical editorial practices, the paper was published without review by any associate editor," that "the subject matter represents" "a significant departure from the nearly purely systematic content" of the journal, and that "there is no credible scientific evidence supporting ID as a testable hypothesis to explain the origin of organic diversity." Richard von Sternberg (available at http://www.rsternberg.net) notes that "typical practice" was neither mandatory nor universally followed. The other two reasons appear to be rooted in pre-judgment of the matter. It is of interest that the concept of a rebuttal to the article was specifically rejected.

[12] Dean Kenyon. A detailed account can be found at J. Myers, "A Scopes Trial in Reverse," (1995, updated 2004). Available at http://www.leaderu.com/real/ri9401/scopes.html.

[13] For examples, see Forrest Mims III, who was rejected as a columnist for *Scientific American* after his creationist beliefs became known (see Mims, "The *Scientific American* Affair," available online at http://www.forrestmims.org/scientificamerican.html), and Robert Gentry, who lost privileges at Oak Ridge National Laboratory after testifying in McLean v. Arkansas, see R. V. Gentry, *Creation's Tiny Mystery* (Knoxville, TN: Earth Science Associates, 2004), especially chapter 13. Available at http://www.halos.com/book/ctm-13-c.htm#4.

[14] A. A. Roth, *Origins: Linking Science and Scripture* (Hagerstown, MD: Review and Herald, 1998), 262–271, has a good presentation of the problem.

[15] See A. A. Roth, "Those Gaps in the Sedimentary Layers," *Origins* 15 (1988): 75–92. Available online at http://www.grisda.org/origins/15075.htm. See also A. A. Roth, *Origins: Linking Science and Scripture,* 222–229.

[16] J. D. Morris, *The Young Earth* (Colorado Springs, CO: Creation-Life Publishers, 1994), 100–102.

[17] Ibid., 106–112. See also A. A. Roth, "Clastic Dikes and Pipes in Kodachrome Basin," *Origins* 19, no. 1 (1992): 44–48. Available online at http://www.grisda.org/origins/19044.htm.

[18] R. H. Brown, "Amino Acid Dating," *Origins* 12 (1988): 8–25. Available online at http://www .grisda.org/origins/12008.pdf.

[19] The major original report was R. H. Vreeland et al., "Isolation of a 250 Million-Year-Old Halotolerant Bacterium From a Primary Salt Crystal," *Nature* 407 (2000): 897–900. There are several other reports and a discussion in the literature, perhaps one of the more significant reports being C. L. Satterfield et al., "New Evidence for 250 Ma Age of Halotolerant Bacterium From a Permian Salt Crystal," *Geology* 33 (2005): 265–268.

[20] The major initial report was M. Schweitzer et al., "Soft-Tissue Vessels and Cellular Preservation in *Tyrannosaurus Rex*," *Science* 307, no. 5717 (2005): 1952–1955. There are several other reports and an active debate in the literature.

[21] Perhaps the definitive exposition of this argument is in J. C. Sanford, *Genetic Entropy and the Mystery of the Genome* (Lima, NY: Elim Publishing, 2005).

[22] A survey of the secular literature can be found in P. Giem, "Carbon-14 Content of Fossil Carbon," *Origins* 51 (2001): 6–30. Available online at http://www.grisda.org/origins/51006.htm. Some striking new data are given in J. Baumgardner, "Carbon-14 Evidence for a Recent Global Flood and a Young Earth," *Radioisotopes and the Age of the Earth: Results of a Young-Earth Creationist Research Initiative,* L. Vardiman, ed., vol. 2 (El Cajon, CA: Institute for Creation Research, 2005), 587–630. Available at http://www.icr.org/article/carbon-14-evidence-for-recent-global.

[23] See P. A. L. Giem, *Scientific Theology* (Riverside, CA: La Sierra University Press, 1997), 188, 189. Available online at http://www.scientifictheology.com.

[24] R. V. Gentry et al., "Radiohalos in Coalified Wood: New Evidence Relating to the Time of Uranium Introduction and Coalification," *Science* 194 (1976): 315–318. Available online at http://www.halos.com/book/ctm-app-07-a.htm.

[25] See P. A. L. Giem (1997). Chapter 5 has a thorough discussion of this approach.

[26] See D. R. Humphreys, "Young Helium Diffusion Age of Zircons Supports Accelerated Nuclear Decay," in *Radioisotopes and the Age of the Earth: Results of a Young-Earth Creationist Research Initiative,* Vardiman, ed., vol. 2 (El Cajon, CA: Institute for Creation Research, 2005), 587–630. Available online at http://www.icr.org/article/young-helium-diffusion-age-zircons.

[27] See A. A. Snelling, "Isochron Discordances and the Rate of Inheritance and Mixing of Radioisotopes in the Mantle and Crust," in *Radioisotopes and the Age of the Earth: Results of a Young-Earth Creationist Research Initiative,* L. Vardiman, ed., vol. 2. (El Cajon, CA: Institute for Creation Research, 2005), 428–434. Available online at http://www.icr.org/article/isochron-discordances-role-inheritance. See also J. Baumgardner (2005), 620, 621.

Chapter 9

Where Did Life Come From?

Life is the most important phenomenon on earth. The biosphere of millions of different kinds of organisms, so extensive that there is not a square inch of sterile surface anywhere on earth, makes the planet pulsate with the many-faceted manifestations of life. But we are a striking singularity in our cosmic neighborhood. After decades of diligent search for life in the solar system, which contains about 150 planets and moons, it is clear that we are alone here.

The question of how life originated on earth is one of the most perplexing puzzles of contemporary science for the following reasons:

1. The works of Redi, Spallanzani, Pasteur, and others conclusively discredited the concept that living matter may spontaneously arise from nonliving matter.
2. The immense isolation of the solar system from other heavenly bodies renders the concept of life being imported from elsewhere in the universe to be beyond the realm of plausibility.

3. Laboratory experiments to generate life from nonliving matter in the past fifty years have not only been utterly unsuccessful but show little promise to ever succeed.
4. Scientists cannot restore dead organisms to life.
5. Analysis of the essence of life reveals that it could not have originated spontaneously anywhere in the universe.

In this discussion, "life" refers to the complex behavior of cells, the fundamental units of living matter. Thus, life is not an abstract entity, but the consequence of thousands of coordinated biochemical processes within the cell. In multicellular beings, living cells constitute living tissues and organs, which in turn are parts of living organisms. The life of a cell is a qualitatively different term than the life of a tissue, an organ, or an organism, though they are related to each other hierarchically. That is, living organisms depend on their living organs and tissues which, in turn, depend on their living cells. In this sense, the term *life* has multiple meanings.

What follows is a more detailed consideration of the five points above. The surprising conclusion will be that the only logical answer to life's origin can be found not in the latest science journals, but in records penned some thirty-five hundred years ago, long before the advent of modern science.

Spontaneous generation of life

From antiquity until the seventeenth century it was commonly held that under favorable conditions, some life forms could arise spontaneously. One "formula" intended to produce mice was to place corn husks and some sweaty underwear in an open bottle for twenty-one days. It was thought that the mud on pond bottoms produced frogs and snakes. Rotten meat supposedly gave rise to maggots.

In 1668 Francesco Redi, an Italian physician and a poet, covered a jar of rotten meat with a fine Naples veil, thus preventing the appearance of maggots. However, in 1745 John Needham, a British biologist and a priest who was a proponent of spontaneous generation of life, took recently boiled beef broth, placed it in a flask, and within days it became cloudy. This was done to demonstrate the spontaneous appearance of microorganisms in broths, which had been sterilized by boiling. In 1768 another Italian physician, Lazzaro Spallanzani repeated Needham's experiment, with the modification that he sealed the flask in which the beef broth was boiled. The broth remained clear until he broke the neck of the flask. Finally, in 1859 the French chemist Louis Pasteur repeated Spallanzani's experiment, except that he stored the boiled broth in flasks with open necks which curved downward, preventing air borne particles to fall into the broth. The broths stayed clear until the bottlenecks were broken. Pasteur's work effectively put an end to the concept of spontaneous generation of life.

Curiously, also in 1859, Charles Darwin's book *On the Origin of Species* was published. Although the treatise does not deal with the question of how the first living organism came into existence, the theory of evolution strongly implied the process of abiogenesis—the generation of life from inorganic matter.

Since Pasteur's work apparently closed the door on the concept of natural abiogenesis, alternative possibilities were then considered in order to account for the appearance of life on earth. One such concept proposed in the early twentieth century was panspermia, the notion that life came to earth from elsewhere in the universe in the form of spores. Eminent Swedish physical chemist Svante Arrhenius was one of the early proponents of this theory.

Search for life in space

Panspermia can occur only if there is a source of living organisms somewhere in outer space, preferably in the solar system. A promising candidate for life-source was Mars, our planetary neighbor, a mere thirty-six million miles away at its closest approach. With temperatures as warm as 20 °C (70 °F), and an atmosphere consisting largely of carbon dioxide, it was envisioned that anaerobic microorganisms ("extremophiles") might exist there, provided there was some water in the soil. In 1976, two fully equipped robotic laboratories landed on Mars as part of the billion-dollar Viking missions. The experiments conducted on Martian soil yielded shocking results. Not only was there no trace of life on Mars, but not a single organic molecule could be found on the Red Planet![1]

Other candidates for life-source in the solar system include Europa, one of Jupiter's moons, believed to possess a subsurface ocean underneath its icy crust, as well as Titan, one of Saturn's moons, which is covered with an extensive atmosphere of nitrogen. Having no further data at this time (2010), we can assert that we are alone in the solar system.

Traveling from the sun at the speed of light, four and a half hours gets us to the outer reaches of the solar system. At this point, we must continue for 4.3 years before reaching the nearest star, Alpha Centauri, which is twenty-five trillion miles away. Thus, we find that Earth is at the center of an imaginary sphere that has a radius of twenty-five trillion miles totally devoid of life. This eliminates the remotest likelihood of panspermia.

Chemical evolution

If panspermia is impossible, the only alternative for evolutionists is abiogenesis on earth. A. I. Oparin wrote,

> By his experiments Pasteur demonstrated beyond peradventure of doubt the impossibility of autogeneration of life in the sense as it was imagined by his predecessors. He showed that living organisms couldn't be formed suddenly before our eyes from formless solutions and infusions. A careful survey of the experimental evidence, however, tells us nothing about the impossibility of generation of life at some other epoch or under some other conditions.[2]

On the one hand, such reasoning downplays the significance of experimentally proven facts. On the other hand, it elevates hypothetical suppositions of what could have happened "in a different epoch." This represents one of the staples of evolutionary reasoning. Thus, in spite of knowing that spontaneous generation of life was an impossibility, in the 1920s British biologist J. B. S. Haldane and Russian chemist, A. I. Oparin, proposed that life on earth probably originated in a primordial ocean where the atmosphere did not contain oxygen.

In the 1920s biochemistry was still in its infancy. Due to lack of information, no one comprehended the enormous complexity of living matter. The first enzyme crystal, made of pure protein, was obtained only in 1926. The citric acid cycle, one of the main metabolic engines of most cells, was discovered in 1937. The general structure of the genetic material, deoxyribonucleic acid (DNA), became known in 1953. Molecular biology came onto the scene in the 1960s, and it was in 1997 when Dolly the sheep was cloned.[3] Therefore, Haldane and Oparin may be excused when they imagined that some simple protoplasmic blobs, precursors of today's organisms, could by chance come into existence in an imagined "primordial" world.

Chemical evolution as a scientific discipline began in 1953, when Stanley Miller, a graduate student at the University of Chicago, set about to test Oparin's hypothesis in the laboratory. He circulated the putative primordial atmospheric gases—water vapor, methane, and ammonia—in a closed glass apparatus and then exposed them to electric discharges. After a week, this procedure yielded four amino acids and numerous other organic compounds.[4]

Soon many variations of the Miller experiment were performed in numerous laboratories, producing most of the twenty amino acids, four nucleo-bases, and sugars and fatty acids, which are the building blocks of the important biological polymers. By the 1970s eagerness to discover the genesis of life of earth reached its zenith. In 1974 Stanley Miller wrote,

> We are confident that the basic process [of chemical evolution] is correct, so confident that it seems inevitable that a similar process has taken place on many other planets of the solar system. . . . We are sufficiently confident of our idea about the origin of life that

in 1976 a spacecraft will be sent to Mars to land on the surface
with the primary purpose of the experiments being a search for
living organisms.[5]

The negative outcome of these experiments has been described above.

Proteins, the most vital components of cells, are composed of strings
of hundreds of amino acid "residues" in specific order. (When a link is
formed between amino acids, a water molecule is lost, and the "residue"
is what is left from the amino acid in the protein.) How amino acids may
polymerize into proteins in aqueous medium, in putative primordial
settings, is yet to be solved.

Meanwhile, in the 1980s it was discovered that some ribonucleic
acids (RNA-s) have enzymatic activities. This discovery pivoted chemical
evolutionary thinking toward the suggestion that life on earth began in
an "RNA World."[6] This concept was reinforced when it was found that
ribosomes, where proteins are made in the cell, are in fact, "ribozymes."
That is, a RNA component in the ribosome catalyzes the linkage
formation between amino acids.

Experimentation, however, revealed the near impossibility of
the routine formation, in a "primordial" setting, of nucleotides, the
nucleobase-ribose-phosphate complexes, which are the building blocks
of ribonucleic acids. One of the current concepts under investigation is
that preceding the "RNA World" there was a simpler genetic system in
play, perhaps composed of self-replicating clay or amino acid-nucleobase
polymers, which "invented" RNA.

Once self-replicating RNA molecules formed, they "invented"
proteins, which in turn, "invented" deoxyribonucleic acids, the modern

genetic material. Darwinian selection created and preserved biologically useful polymers, and this is how the first living cells came into existence.

This narrative assigns the invention and production of the thousands of molecular machines necessary for living matter to a hypothetical self-replicating system capable of mutation. It ignores the essential fact that only living matter is capable of discriminating between useful and non-useful substances.

Given that even the first steps of this version of chemical evolution are without experimental foundation, after more than fifty years of valiant struggle in the laboratory, the entire concept of chemical evolution is on the verge of extinction.

Restoring dead cells to life

In the course of my laboratory work with *Escherichia coli,* I treated liquid cultures with toluene, a substance which dissolves the lipids of the outer and inner membranes of *E. coli,* killing them. We now know the chemical composition of *E. coli,* as well as the exact sequence of its 4.6-million nucleotide chromosome, and the functions of 75 percent of its 4,290 proteins. Yet, with all this information, we are still unable to restore to life dead *E. coli* cells. The strange thing is that the dead cells closely resemble the live cells in cellular chemical composition—it's just that there are some holes in the membranes of the dead cells.

What is the essence of life?

Leaky membranes in *E. coli* prevent energy generation. In the absence of chemical energy, supplied by adenosine triphosphate molecules (ATP), biochemical pathways shut down and the cells die. Life processes depend on chemical changes. Isolated chemical reactions routinely reach their end points—equilibria—at which point chemical changes cease. This does not happen in live cells because chemical reactions are connected into pathways. The products of pathways are either utilized by the cell's metabolism or, if they begin to accumulate, the pathways shut down through sophisticated regulatory mechanisms. Living matter requires the presence of the genetic material and thousands of specific proteins; however, these are also present in the toluene-killed *E. coli* cells.

At the time of death there is no measurable change in the complexity of *E. coli*. With the passage of time, the intricate cellular makeup will degrade; however, seconds after death, the sole difference between a live and a dead cell is the equilibrium states of the reactions and pathways. The irreducible complexity of living matter, so elegantly explained by Michael Behe,[7] is unaltered when equilibrium sets in. Therefore, while irreducible complexity maybe necessary for living matter to exist, it is insufficient to explain life.

It is the non-equilibrium status of the thousands of chemical reactions that keep the cells alive. Any scheme positing that living matter comes into existence piecemeal, step by step, must deal with this insurmountable problem: how to convert large numbers of chemical reactions from their equilibrium states to non-equilibria.

The famous La Chatelier's principle states, If a chemical system at equilibrium experiences a change in concentration, temperature, volume, or partial pressure, then the equilibrium shifts to counteract the imposed change. This principle ensures the impossibility of the spontaneous reversal of dead cells to life. It also nullifies any chemical evolutionary scheme on earth, as well as anywhere in the universe.

Conclusion

There is only one correct answer possible to the question "Where did life come from?" It is not found in the review articles of scientific journals, nor in biology textbooks. The answer is given by the Creator Himself, etched in stone by His fingers (Exodus 31:18). "For in six days the Lord made the heavens and the earth, the sea, and all that is in them" (Exodus 20:11).

For further reading:

Javor, G. T., *Evidences for Creation.* Hagerstown, MD: Review and Herald Publishing Association, 2005.

Thaxton, C. B., Bradley, W. L., and Olsen, R. I., *The Mystery of Life's Origin: Reassessing Current Theories.* New York: Philosophical Library, 1984.

Behe, M., *Darwin's Black Box: The Biochemical Challenge to Evolution.* New York: Free Press, 1996.

Meyer, S. C., *Signature in the Cell.* New York: HarperCollins Publishers, 2009.

George Javor is professor emeritus of Loma Linda University School of Medicine. He received his ScB in chemistry from Brown University and a PhD degree in biochemistry from Columbia University. Following postdoctoral research at Rockefeller University, he joined the Chemistry Department at Andrews University. After eleven years he transferred to the Microbiology Department of Loma Linda University, where he spent twenty-six years teaching medical, dental, and graduate students and pursuing basic research on the physiology of Escherichia coli. He published several articles in peer-reviewed scientific journals and in denominational publications, and also three books.

References

[1] S. A. Benner et al., "The Missing Organic Molecules on Mars," *Proceedings of the National Academy of Sciences* 97, no. 6 (2000): 2425–2430.

[2] A. I. Oparin, *The Origins of Life,* Sergius Morgulis, trans. (Mineola, NY: Dover Publications, 1953), 29.

[3] I. Wilmut et al., "Viable Offspring Derived From Fetal and Adult Mammalian Cells," *Nature* 385, no. 6619 (1997): 810–813, doi:10.1038/385810a0. PMID 9039911.

[4] Stanley L. Miller, "Production of Amino Acids Under Possible Primitive Earth Conditions," *Science* 117, no. 3046 (May 1953): 528, doi:10.1126/science.117.3046.528.

[5] S. I. Miller, *The Heritage of Copernicus* (Cambridge, MA: MIT Press, 1974), 328.

[6] G. F. Joyce, "RNA Evolution and the Origin of Life," *Nature* 338 (1989): 217–224.

[7] M. J. Behe, *Darwin's Black Box* (New York: Free Press, 1996).

Chapter 10

How Reliable Is Radiometric Dating?

The question of how much time is involved for the history of the earth is one of the most contentious issues in discussions of creation and evolution. Two sources of information about the past history (that is, time) of our planet and solar system are available. The biblical record suggests a short period of time, measured in thousands of years, since the creation. The overwhelming majority of scientists maintain that earth's history involves billions of years, during which living organisms somehow arose and then diversified to produce the present flora and fauna. One of the most important arguments for a very ancient world is based on radiometric dating. This chapter will consider the issues a creationist can expect to face when dealing with radiometric dating and the age of the earth.

Scientific details

The scientific aspects of time can be represented by three divisions, with some overlap: (1) an absolute time scale, (2) relative time scales, and

(3) physical and chemical time scales. The dating methods that yield the physical time scale are based on atomic changes that are dependent only on time, with environmental factors such as temperature and pressure expected to have no influence.

Most chronostratigraphic (sequential earth layer ages) time scales are based on ages obtained with physical methods, the most important of which uses radioactive decay. The methods used do not necessarily yield absolute dates because geophysical and geochemical processes complicate the model conditions for age determination. For example, the radiocarbon time scale has deviations from the absolute time scale. Chronostratigraphic ages are given the name of the method so their limitations can be taken into account, for example, the potassium/argon age.

In radioactive decay, certain isotopes (kinds of atoms) are unstable and disintegrate. An unstable parent atom decays into a stable daughter atom and a subatomic particle that can damage nearby atoms. The decay process occurs at a rate that follows a mathematical formula such that half of the parent atoms decay into daughter atoms in a fixed period of time known as the half-life. Different unstable isotopes have different half-lives. For example, the half-life of radioactive potassium-40 is about 1.26 billion years, while the half-life of radioactive uranium-238 is about 4.47 billion years. In contrast, the time required for half a sample of neodymium-142 to decay is about 100,000 years. For dating purposes, the half-life must be short enough to have produced a measurable amount of daughter isotope since time zero of the sample being studied. It must also be long enough that a measurable amount of parent isotope is still present. The age of a sample is calculated from the amounts of parent material and daughter material using the appropriate mathematical formula.

The birth of modern geochronology was presaged at the end of the 1930s by Nier and Mattauch, who invented the mass spectrometer, an instrument measuring the masses of an atom's isotopes. For the first time, isotope abundances could be measured with sufficient accuracy to distinguish nonradiogenic components from radiogenic components. (Isotopes that are not a result of radioactive decay could be distinguished from isotopes that are a result of radioactive decay.) The potential practical applications of this instrument expanded very rapidly, and further developments are still occurring today.

The reliability of radiometric dating depends on the reliability of the assumptions on which it is based. All classical dating methods based on the radioactive decay of natural isotopes with long half-lives (not including carbon-14 dating) use the following model assumptions:

1. *Known initial conditions.* None of the daughter element was present in the mineral or rock at τo (the starting point of the radiometric "clock") or the isotopic composition of the daughter element initially present can be determined reliably, for example, by the isochron (equal in time) method, and is corrected for.
2. *Closed system.* The mineral or rock has formed a closed geochemical system (that is, neither parent nor daughter element has been added or removed) since τo.
3. *Constant decay.* The decay constant λ is truly constant and is known with sufficient accuracy.

Although radiometric dating has weaknesses, they are well-known, and samples are carefully collected to avoid problems. Challenging radiometric dating on the basis of the possible unreliability of its assumptions has not been very successful. Individual dates are often shown to be wrong, but the overall pattern of dates has enough consistency that it seems to represent more than mere chance. We cannot rule out the possibility that something may be systematically wrong with the theory and method of radiometric dating, but we have not been able to identify what that might be.

Biblical constraints

The Scriptural aspects of time are seen in Genesis where general time considerations are first presented, "In the beginning . . ." and then a specific time line for the length or duration of life is outlined after life has been placed on this planet. Seventh-day Adventists have made the conscious choice to accept Creation as revealed in Scripture. This choice comes with a time constraint of six literal days for Creation and a seventh day added for rest and worship. There is a great difference between one week and six hundred million years for the development of life! Even if the genealogies are rounded off or doubled, the time for life on this planet is on the order of thousands or tens of thousands of years, not millions of years.

Having made this choice, we look for alternate interpretations of the chronostratigraphy of the layers of the earth's crust that contain evidence for life. The question becomes, "How do one's time constraints begin to resolve the time issues?" One approach may be as follows:

1. Assume that the creation of the universe and world and the creation of life on this earth are distinct processes occurring at two different times. The first, or primordial, creation occurring in the far distant

past (Genesis 1:1, 2) was followed by the creation of life on earth within the past thousands, not millions, of years (Genesis 1:3 and onward).[1]

2. Assume that the vast number of fossils within the strata of the earth's crust was deposited by a worldwide flood that took place sometime after the creation of life.[2]

3. Accept that the primary purpose for the lineages given in Genesis was to establish the relationship between God and humans and to set the stage for the eventual coming of the Messiah rather than precisely fixing the date of Creation week.

4. Accept the Creation week as establishing God as Creator and the weekly cycle, firmly fixing the seventh day as the Sabbath and a memorial to our God the Creator.

An old solar system

Using this approach we first address the age of inorganic, nonliving matter of the earth and solar system, understanding that the mineral planet might have existed for a long period of time before the creation of life described in Genesis. The fact that we find radioactive isotopes present in the materials from the earth, moon, and meteorites strongly suggests that our solar system has a finite age. Potential minimum and maximum ages for its formation may be obtained through an analysis of radioactive isotopes, parent/daughter ratios, and missing radioactive isotopes.

For example, uranium-238 has a half life of 4.47 billion years. After seven to ten half-lives, the parent isotope is exhausted and there is too little remaining to be detectable. Some uranium-238 still exists, so we can conclude that the solar system has a maximum age of about 45 billion years. This figure is further refined by analyzing the U-235/U-238 ratio, which implies a maximum age of about 5 billion years. Using the same method of analyzing parent/daughter ratios, focusing on the systems where daughter isotopes are found and parent isotopes are clearly absent, a minimum age can be determined for the solar system. For example, samarium-146 with a half-life of about 100 million years is not found in naturally occurring deposits; however, its stable daughter product neodymium-142, is found in abundance. This means the solar system must be no younger than about ten half-lives of neodymium-142, which is about 1 billion years. This process brings us to the interesting conclusion that the radiometric age of the planets, moons, and meteorites of our solar system may range between one and 5 billion years.

When multiple samples analyzed via multiple isotope techniques agree, they are said to be concordant. Concordant dates cannot be easily rejected and often point to physically significant events. The concordance observed between the numerous radiometric age determinations for the formation of our solar system yields an age of 4.56 billion years.

Can life on earth be young?

What options are available for interpreting the matter of the solar system and earth as being old, but yet life on earth as being young? One approach is to suggest that the modern stratigraphic ages for the fossil layers are accepted only as the result of a worldview in which there is no time constraint. This approach goes on to question the reliability of some of the methods and assumptions used in the radiometric dating of the earth's fossil layers. The assumption of constant, known decay rates is probably reliable, especially with today's technology; however, the other two assumptions recognized by the practitioners of radiometric dating, namely known initial conditions (complete resetting of the "clock") and a closed system, are not always fulfilled.[3] Following are some possible questions about the methods and assumptions of radiometric dating:

1. *Interpretation.* No simple, applicable procedures are available for interpreting dating results. The conditions at the sampling site, the composition, the origin of the sample, and the preparation techniques in the laboratory are decisive for the interpretation of the results. Each case must be considered separately and requires a specific model with defined limiting conditions. Often complicated mathematical models must be developed.

2. *Model ages.* A distinction is made between true, model, apparent, and conventional ages. The word *model* indicates that the age is derived from material properties within the framework of a specific set of contextual and geochemical-geophysical assumptions and constraints. If these assumptions are fulfilled, the age is called a "true" model age. If not, "apparent" model ages are obtained. Conventional ages are determined according to international guidelines; these are C-14, K/Ar, Rb/Sr, and U-Th/Pb methods. Conventional ages are considered the most precise of all dates determined by physical methods and can be compared better than others.

3. *Isochron or magma mixing line.* Radiometric ages are often derived from a set of graphed data points that define a straight line called an

isochron. The age of the rock is calculated from the slope of this line with steeper lines yielding older ages. However, the linear data points may result from the mixing of two different magmas instead of from radioactive decay. It is often difficult to distinguish an isochron from a mixing line, although various possibilities are available.[4] When more than one isotope method yields the same or nearly the same (concordant) date, the likelihood of it being a real age increases. Concordance is not uncommon when dealing with the inorganic matter of the earth but may be less common when calculating the dates of fossil material.

4. *Discordance.* Scientists performing more than one calculation of radiometric age on a given sample are not surprised when the resulting ages disagree. This disagreement implies that the sample under study may have experienced more than one age-altering event. Such events may include solidification, heating, remelting, severe shock, mixing with other materials, and exposure to water or high energy radiation. These events affect (or even reset) different isotopes in the same sample in different ways. Therefore discordance may provide useful insight into the chronology of events that the sample has experienced.[5]

5. *Nonresetting.* The radiometric clocks may not be reset to zero when the minerals are transported by erosional or igneous processes. Because erosional and other sedimentary processes rarely reset the clock, radiometric dating is rarely used to date sedimentary rocks such as sandstones, shales, and limestones; however, granitic,

volcanic, and metamorphic rocks that have undergone igneous processes are often used for radiometric dating. This option suggests that the radiometric ages assigned to the inorganic minerals associated with a fossil are more a reflection of the characteristics of the source material than an indication of the age of the fossil. The nonreset problems for radiometric ages are not hidden nor are they ignored within the scientific community, for many illustrations are found in the scientific literature documenting such problems.

6. *Contamination.* Contamination is another problem that arises when dealing with radiometric age determinations. The extent to which contamination affects the various methods can differ greatly. For example, U-Th dates on stalactites or stalagmites may be too large by many thousands of years without any indication that such error exists. The cause can be clay that contains traces of Th-239 or the leaching of uranium.[6]

7. *Other.* Deviations occur as a result of other processes as well. Such processes can be geochemical or geophysical, for example, diagenetic mobilization (a complex process that changes newly deposited sediments into rock) of parent or daughter nuclides in a mineral or rock system, the occurrence or annealing of radiation damage, isotope fractionation (unequal distribution of isotopes), or long-term fluctuations in the production of cosmogenic radionuclides (radioactive elements, such as C-14, that are continually produced in the earth's upper atmosphere).

Conclusion

Time is real only because man is finite. However, all aspects of mankind's interpretation of time may not be real. Therefore we should exercise caution whenever attempting to enforce a rigid interpretation of a prehistoric phenomenon, irrespective of the data, be it science or Scripture. The biblical record does not address the age questions directly. The biggest difficulty for the scriptural interpretation of the age of the earth is the progressive radiometric ages found within the geologic column. There does not seem to be any direct linear relationship between the radiometric time observed throughout the geologic column and the lineages of Scripture.

Given this difficulty, and the significance of faith in the scriptural account, we would do well to recognize the limitations of our knowledge, maintaining our faith as the highest priority while humbly acknowledging the tension that remains between our understanding of the Bible and our understanding of science. We must remember, however, that an old age for the physical earth does not directly imply an old age for life.

Clyde L. Webster Jr. completed a chemistry major at Walla Walla College and received his PhD in physical inorganic geochemistry from Colorado State University. He served as chair of the Chemistry Department at Loma Linda University, Riverside, and also at Walla Walla College prior to joining the Geoscience Research Institute in 1983. He has published several articles and has traveled worldwide participating in numerous seminars on faith and science until 2000, when due to health concerns he retired from full-time employment. Currently, he is a visiting professor at the University of California, Riverside, and a research professor at La Sierra University.

References

[1] F. D. Nichol, "How Old Is the Earth?" *Review and Herald,* December 3, 1964.

[2] Nichol, "How Old Is the Earth?"

[3] For example, E. Heath et al., "Long Magma Residence Times at an Island Arc Volcano (Soufriere, St. Vincent) in the Lesser Antilles: Evidence From 238U-230 Th Isochron Dating," *Earth and Planetary Science Letters* 160 (1998): 49–63.

[4] For example, see R. J. Fleck and R. E. Criss, "Strontium and Oxygen Isotopic Variations in Mesosoic and Tertiary Plutons of Central Idaho," *Contributions to Mineralogy and Petrology* 90 (1985): 291–308.

[5] For example, Joachim Pilot et al., "Palaeozoic and Proterozoic Zircons From the Mid-Atlantic Ridge," *Nature* 393 (June 18, 1998): 676–679.

[6] Robert M. Garrels and Charles L. Christ, *Solutions, Minerals, and Equilibria* (New York, NY: Harper & Row, 1965), 253.

Chapter 11

Can I Believe in a Worldwide Flood?

The Flood described in Genesis is both momentous and astonishing. The Bible devotes three entire chapters to describing it—longer than the two narrating the Creation account. We can find significant authentication for the Flood beyond the biblical account.

In a biblical context, the Genesis flood event reconciles a recent creation to the majority of the worldwide fossil record. Some suggest that the Genesis flood was a local event, or that it only produced a small portion of the fossil record, but such suggestions do not agree with the biblical account indicating that "all the high hills that were under the whole heaven were covered" (Genesis 7:19, KJV). Moreover, unless conditions were very different from the ordinary, it seems unlikely that major portions of the fossil record could have formed in the relatively short time before and after the Flood. The biblical model appears to be that of a recent six-day creation and a catastrophic worldwide flood accounting for much of the fossil record. This model stands in stark contrast to the evolutionary model of the fossil record representing gradual evolutionary development of life over billions of years.

It is not necessary to rely on the biblical account to find support for the reality of a Flood. The concept is well documented in the world's traditions and folk literature. Accounts of a worldwide flood are six times as common as other kinds of past worldwide calamities (table 1). In Stith Thompson's monumental six-volume treatise on folk literature,[1] there are 122 references to a worldwide flood. Fire is the next most common cause of a past worldwide calamity, with 19 references. Earthquakes, volcanoes, pestilence, and drought are not mentioned. Some try to explain folk flood accounts as based on numerous local floods occurring over time developing before broader communication facilitated confirmation of worldwide events. However, if there had been many local events occurring over time, we would expect mention of a great variety of causes. A reasonable conclusion is that the dominance of worldwide flood accounts simply results from the occurrence of an actual flood event of such magnitude that it was memorable to many peoples, and thus remained preserved in their oral histories.

Table 1
References to world calamities in folk literature
(Exclusive of end-of-world calamities. Based on Thompson, 1955)

Causes	Number of references
Deluge (worldwide flood)	122
Fire	19
Continuous winter	6
Large stones	2
Ogre	1
Earthworm	1
Objects (dead and alive)	1
Sunrise	1

Geologists in general completely reject the Genesis flood interpretation; however, during the last half century a new trend has allowed catastrophes such as major floods into geologic interpretations. These new interpretations often include conclusions that coincide to a great degree with the results that would be expected from a worldwide flood. If such a flood were responsible for much of the fossil and accompanying sedimentary record, it would be expected that significant evidence for this should be found, which is, in fact, the case. Several lines of geological evidence favoring the Flood follow.

Ocean sediments on the continents. The sediments on the continents, which contain most of the fossils, show an average thickness of about 1.5 kilometers—about four times the present thickness of sediments on the ocean floor, where rivers now deposit sediments. A further surprising fact is that about half of the sediments on the continents contain fossils of marine organisms. Why is there such a great quantity of ocean material on the continents? Many geologists explain this by positing that epicontinental seas were formed on continents in the past due to repeated flooding. This may be precisely what the Genesis flood was all about!

Abundant rapid underwater activity on the continents. One of the breakthroughs in the interpretation of sediments has been recognition of the commonness of rapid underwater deposition in the rock record, which is preserved in the form of turbidites, massive underwater landslides, and other similar rapid processes. These features are exactly what would be expected during a global flood.

Evidence of continental-scale currents. Another interesting feature is that many sedimentary layers show a dominant continent-wide direction of flow as they were deposited at various levels[2]—also to be expected during a worldwide flood. For example, Paleozoic rocks in North America show a predominant trend from northeast to southwest, with little apparent topographical influence.

Widespread sedimentary deposits. As one examines the crust of the earth, one is struck by the fact that many unique sedimentary deposits are extremely flat and widespread over major parts of continents. It would take very forceful events indeed to lay down such unique layers. One geologist who does not accept the Genesis flood describes the cause of these as "extreme events . . . with magnitudes so large and devastating that they have not, and probably could not, be observed scientifically."[3] Such events would have had worldwide consequences. Figure 1 illustrates two examples of widespread deposits. The very thin whitish layer just above the tip of the arrow, the Cretaceous Dakota Formation, which has varied layers, averages only about 30 meters in thickness but is spread over some 815,000 square kilometers in the western United States.

Producing such a formation requires extremely flat topography or surface. The darker layers, just below the tip of the arrow, are the famous Jurassic Morrison Formation, especially noted for its dinosaur fossils. It averages around one hundred meters in thickness and extends from Texas in the southern part of the United States all the way north into Canada, covering one million square kilometers. No evidence of a major river has been found in the entire Morrison Formation.[4] We see nothing like this widespread deposition occurring on our continents at this time. However,

40 million

Figure 1. Geologic layers at Continental Divide, New Mexico. The layer just above the tip of the arrow is the Dakota Formation, the layer just below is the Morrison Formation; between the two a putative gap of some forty million years of the geologic column is missing, yet the contact surface is very flat.

such large-scale geologic deposition represents precisely the type of activity we would expect from a major catastrophic Flood.

Flat gaps in the sedimentary layers. In many parts of the world, we often find major parts of the geologic column missing between the sedimentary layers with no evidence of the passing of time. In these places, sedimentary layers were simply not deposited. The usual explanation is that these were upland areas, not basins where sediments would tend to accumulate. According to the long geologic ages model, these gaps represent millions of years. If those long ages had actually occurred, we would expect a great deal of erosion of these uplands. Erosion usually leaves an irregular surface, but the topography at these gaps is remarkably flat, indicating little or no time for erosion at the gaps.[5] Geologists call these flat gaps paraconformities or disconformities.

The arrow in figure 1 points to one of those flat gaps where the top part of the Jurassic and the bottom part of the Cretaceous periods of the geologic column are missing between the Morrison and Dakota formations. According to the geologic time scale, this represents a gap of about forty million years. At average rates of erosion for the world's continents,[6] we would expect the removal of more than a kilometer of depth of sediments during that time. Nevertheless, we can see that the contact between the two layers is very flat, as though they had been laid down in rapid succession. This gap is widespread over hundreds of thousands of square kilometers in the western United States. A little erosion is seen very rarely, but this would be expected during a flood. These flat gaps challenge the assumed millions of years of the geologic column, and testify to the rapid deposition of the sedimentary record as expected for the Flood.

Incomplete ecological systems. Almost all animals directly or indirectly require plants for survival. When we find major areas in the fossil record with many animals and few or no plants, it leads us to wonder how the animals survived over the millions of years postulated for the deposition of the sedimentary layers involved. We seem to have evidence of incomplete ecological systems where animals would not have been able to survive due to a lack of food. Such conditions fit better with a catastrophic flood model, where moving waters would have separated animals from plants, the latter becoming transformed into some of our extensive coal deposits.

The Morrison Formation mentioned above appears to be just one of those huge but incomplete ecological systems. It has been one of the world's richest sources of dinosaur fossils, yet plants are rare. What did these behemoths eat? The paleontologist Theodor White comments that "although the Morrison was an area of reasonably rapid accumulation of sediment, identifiable plant fossils are practically nonexistent."[7] A similar situation exists in Mongolia's Gobi Desert, and in the Coconino Sandstone of the southwestern United States.[8] In the latter case, there appear to be no plants, yet there are hundreds of animal trackways almost all going uphill,[9] as though the animals were fleeing rising floodwaters.

Unusual coal deposits. Some fossil coal seams are immense, covering thousands of square kilometers and reaching 150 meters in thickness. We do not find such large deposits of coal currently being formed on earth—only a limited amount in peat bogs and swamps. The usually sharp contacts and uniform thickness of the fossil coal seams, as well as the many repeated cycles of deposition fit well with idea of rapid flood deposition. Furthermore, the presence of sedimentary layers called "partings" just a few centimeters thick, sometimes spread over a thousand square kilometers within a coal seam,[10] seems best explained as the result of water transport. During the Flood, flowing water would be expected to separate out the lighter floating vegetation that would eventually become vast coal layers.

Scientific data challenging long geologic ages. A significant body of scientific data indicates that the billions of years proposed for the geologic layers is invalid. While this data does not validate the Flood as directly as the evidence described above, it nevertheless lends solid support to a recent biblical flood as compared to the long, slow evolutionary model. Several examples of the data are listed and described below.

1. The erosion rates of our continents are so rapid that the continents could have been eroded to sea level more than one hundred times during the billions of years proposed for their existence.[11]

2. Carbon-14, which decays relatively rapidly, should not be detected at all in samples older than a million years. Yet nearly a hundred samples, including some diamonds assumed to be millions to hundreds of millions of years old, show significant carbon-14, which suggests a much younger age.[12]

3. Archaeological evidence for writing and major architectural developments, such as aqueducts and pyramids, is only a few thousand years old. According to evolutionary interpretations, the genus *Homo* is thought to have existed for more than two million years, and *Homo sapiens* for two hundred to perhaps five hundred thousand years. Why would humanity take so long to achieve such advances?[13]

4. The human population will soon reach seven billion, and based on the most recent data, is doubling in size in much less than one hundred years. While varied factors have been invoked to explain the existence of slower rates in the past, cautious estimates based on present rates indicate it would take only a few thousand years to generate a population of seven billion, starting with just two parents. If humankind is ancient, as commonly suggested, it seems that the earth should have been full a long time ago.

5. Mutations are notoriously harmful. Calculations indicate that, because of the high mutation rate found in humans, the human race should have degenerated to the point of extinction long ago. If humans have existed as long as geologic time suggests, how have we survived against such harmful odds?[14]

6. Scientists have found soft, fresh-looking tissue in dinosaurs purportedly eighty million years old.[15] Protein molecules are not expected to survive one hundred thousand years, but have nevertheless been found in a variety of fossils from various parts of the geologic column.

7. The billions of years of geologic time are far *too short* to support the improbabilities of evolution, such as producing even one specific protein molecule, let alone the first form of life that would be very complex.[16]

Conclusion

A significant body of scientific data is quite difficult to explain unless one believes the biblical flood account. The folk literature, geological data, other corroborating scientific data, and the Bible itself all authenticate that astonishing catastrophe.

Ariel A. Roth earned his PhD in zoology from the University of Michigan. He has served on the faculty of Andrews and Loma Linda Universities, as well as director of the Geoscience Research Institute, where he initiated the journal Origins. *In the evolution-creation controversy, he has served as consultant, witness, and keynote speaker for the states of California, Arkansas, and Oregon. He has published more than 180 articles in both scientific and popular journals. His book* Origins: Linking Science and Scripture *is published in sixteen languages, and his new book,* Science Discovers God, *is now available in seven languages.*

References

[1] S. Thompson, *Motif Index of Folk Literature,* rev. ed. (Bloomington, IN: Indiana University Press, 1955).

[2] A. V. Chadwick, "Megatrends in North American Paleocurrents," *Society of Economic Paleontologists and Mineralogists Abstracts with Programs* 8 (1993): 58.

[3] Carlton E. Brett, "A Slice of the 'Layer Cake': The Paradox of 'Frosting Continuity,'" *Palaios* 15 (2000): 495–498.

[4] P. Dodson et al., "Taphonomy and Paleoecology of the Dinosaur Beds of the Jurassic Morrison Formation," *Paleobiology* 6 (1980): 208–232.

[5] For further details, see A. A. Roth, "'Flat Gaps' in Sedimentary Rock Layers Challenge Long Geologic Ages," *Journal of Creation* 23, no. 2 (2009): 76–81. A. A. Roth, "Those Gaps in the Sedimentary Layers," *Origins* 15 (1988): 75–92.

[6] Ancient rates of erosion are estimated to be around half to one-third slower than present ones because of man's agricultural practices. The estimate given adjusts for this.

[7] T. E. White, "The Dinosaur Quarry," in *Guidebook to the Geology and Mineral Resources of the Uinta Basin,* E. F. Sabatka, ed. (Salt Lake City: Intermountain Association of Geologists, 1964), 21–28.

[8] For details and references, see A. A. Roth, *Origins: Linking Science and Scripture* (Hagerstown, MD: Review and Herald, 1998), 219–222.

[9] C. W. Gilmore, "Fossil Footprints From the Grand Canyon: Second Contribution," *Smithsonian Miscellaneous Collections* 80, no. 3 (1927): 1–78.

[10] S. A. Austin, "Evidence of Marine Origin of Widespread Carbonaceous Shale Partings in the Kentucky No. 12 Coal Bed (Middle Pennsylvanian) of Western Kentucky," *Geological Society of America, Abstracts With Programs* 11, no. 7 (1979): 381, 382.

[11] For calculations, see Roth (1998), 263–266, 271–273.

[12] P. Giem, "Carbon-14 Content of Fossil Carbon," *Origins* 51 (2001): 6–30.

[13] Roth (1998), 124.

[14] T. Beardsley, "Mutations Galore: Humans Have High Mutation Rates. But Why Worry?" *Scientific American* 280, no. 4 (1999): 32, 36; J. C. Sanford, *Genetic Entropy & the Mystery of the Genome* (Waterloo, NY: FMS Publications, 2008).

[15] M. H. Schweitzer, "Biomolecular Characterization and Protein Sequences of the Campanian Hadrosaur *B. Canadensis,*" *Science* 324 (2009): 626–631.

[16] A. A. Roth, *Science Discovers God: Seven Convincing Lines of Evidence for His Existence* (Hagerstown, MD: Autumn House Publishing, 2009), 85–88, 138–142.

Chapter 12

What Does the Fossil Record Tell Us?

The fossil record is an archive showing the history of life on earth. It includes related data, for example the nature of the rock layers in which it is found. Researchers have developed an impressively large database[1] containing not only raw data but also interpretations about the remains, rocks, processes, time involved, and the supposed ecology of those organisms. It is important to keep in mind that the database contains both objective data and interpretations of it.

How well-known is the fossil record? A recent study[2] has shown that when the fossil collector's curves[3] are analyzed, the number of fossil vertebrate and invertebrate families described during the past two hundred years shows a continuous increase to more than three thousand families at present. On the other hand, the number of families with both fossil and living representatives has leveled off at about sixteen hundred families. This suggests that the global Phanerozoic (that is, current geologic era) record of fossil metazoans (multicellular organisms) is still fairly incomplete; however, it is believed that the known record is quite representative.

When considering the available data, great care should be taken in making interpretations and constructing arguments to support our views. In the next section we discuss some widely held views that are not supported by the data.

Dispelling erroneous conceptions

As Christian scientists and students, we need to be on the lookout for "bad science"—claims that are unsupported by either data or the Scriptures. Examples of erroneous ideas that have been promoted by some creationists are listed below.

Misconception 1: The geologic or stratigraphic (rock layer) column is not real, but is a human construct intended to mislead us. We noted earlier that the record is real, the data are real, and in spite of problems with some interpretations, the overall stratigraphic sequence is real. Problems arise from differences in interpretation regarding the origin of the observed sequence or the nature of the processes that produced the sequence. How could there be order, some ask, if everything resulted from a major catastrophe such as a global flood? However, experience in the field consistently shows that order is present in the fossil record. This very consistency in the ordered sequence is the reason for the success of various geological exploration technologies that are used in the exploitation of mineral and fossil resources.

Misconception 2: Fossil reconstructions are full of errors. In the first years of paleontology as a science, many errors were committed as organisms were reconstructed based on very few fossil bones, or when parts that had been discovered were assigned to a particular organism. However, today's reconstructions have become quite accurate due to the development of various subspecialties and the discovery of vast numbers of remains on all continents.

Misconception 3: Dinosaurs are not real. Today, nearly everyone recognizes that dinosaurs really existed.[4] Paleontologists as well as dinosaur enthusiasts have found thousands of dinosaur fossils, including eggs and embryos, and recently, organic molecules, such as the protein collagen, and what appear to be well-preserved blood and bone cells and blood vessels.

Misconception 4: There are human footprints alongside those of dinosaurs. This notion became very popular (in some places remains so) based on claims of such a discovery in the bedrock at Paluxy River, Texas. What is not well-known is that Seventh-day Adventist creation scientists were the ones who put the evidence to the test and discovered the fraudulent nature of the human track claims. One must be wary of claims publicized as "proofs" that are necessary to sustain our beliefs.

Misconception 5: The entire fossil record or geologic column was laid down during the one year of the biblical flood. Some may have envisioned the formation of the geologic column as result of a single catastrophic event, but we now know that the record is more complex than a single event could produce. Based on the data, a reasonable scenario suggests that part of the lower portion of the record consists of pre-Flood rocks that were not completely altered or eroded away by the catastrophe. In the same way, an upper part of the section most likely represents the strata and processes that occurred after the Flood. In this way a significant amount of geological activity would be represented in the "pre-Flood" and the "post-Flood" rocks.

Misconception 6: Marine fossils high in the mountains are proof that the floodwaters covered the highest peaks and therefore the whole earth. Those fossils were not strewn around the mountain peaks as the water covered them, but were produced when organisms died in a body of water (or were washed in) and were then covered with layers of sediment. Later, those layers were uplifted during mountain-forming processes. The fossils or the sediments that buried them could have been a direct result of the Flood or a consequence of Flood-related events.

Misconception 7: The fossil record proves evolution (or proves the biblical flood). We like certainty—the knowledge that we have the right answers or beliefs. Unfortunately science, because of its methods and limitations, does not provide ultimate truth, especially regarding theories such as evolution or Creation, which have a metaphysical component. What it can do is provide evidence for aspects of evolutionary theory, such as the ways in which similar organisms are adapted for different environments, or for catastrophic processes that led to the extinction of some life forms.

Evidence consistent with a short-age geological model that considers data from the biblical record[5]

We will now consider some of the arguments that earth scientists have proposed in attempting to develop a degree of harmony between the biblical record and the scientific evidence.[6] At present we still experience serious problems with some unresolved questions.

First, we don't yet have a satisfactory overarching detailed model for the development of the geologic column and its fossil record. Hypotheses have been proposed (for example, try to fit all the geologic column in the year of the Flood, or an extended Flood model), but each one has numerous problems and raises more questions than it answers. Nevertheless, some attempts have been made,[7] and this remains an area of active research.

Secondly, some major features of the fossil record are difficult to interpret within a short time frame.[8] These include (1) the existence of fossils with characteristics that appear to be intermediate between recognized groups of species (however, some of these "forms" may have been part of the original creation); (2) the existence of an overall fossil sequence, and even some sequences within certain groups of fossil organisms; (3) the number of fossil families with living representatives, which increases as one moves upward through the geologic column; and (4) some biogeographic distribution patterns that prove difficult to explain.

In spite of these problems, there is abundant evidence suggesting an alternative view to that of conventional geology and paleontology, as described below.

Evidence 1: Geological and paleontological data demonstrate sediment and fossil accumulation through catastrophic processes.

There is increased recognition among mainstream earth scientists that many rock strata have formed catastrophically. Until only a few decades ago, the dominant principle for geological interpretation was that of *uniformitarianism*—the idea that processes in the past occurred at the same rates as they do in the present. However, many have recognized the problems of this influential paradigm and have come to accept the occurrence of many catastrophic events in the geologic past. Examples of catastrophic features include recognition of well-documented megaflood events (Lake Missoula,[9] Mediterranean Sea,[10] British Channel,[11] among others); recognition of turbidites (rock units resulting from high speed subaqueous flows)[12]; rapid accumulation of rhythmites[13]—layers of sedimentary rock laid down with an obvious periodicity—which were previously interpreted as result of slow multiyear deposition or attributed to yearly seasonal deposition, such as varves (layers of sediment deposited in a body of still water in a single year); the influence of large-scale volcanism in rapid burial events (for example, sedimentary accumulation of volcanic ash)[14]; the large-scale effects of bolide impacts[15]—a meteor that hits the earth (an amazing number of asteroids have hit the earth and exploded, causing environmental disruption and destruction of life). One must keep in mind that the fossil record is embedded in rock units possessing these features, showing that the fossils accumulated in catastrophic conditions.

Associated with this evidence of rapid geological activity are many non-uniformitarian features,[16] such as large-scale sedimentary processes (for example, Jurassic Morrison Formation and associated rock units); global distribution of marine rocks (with extensive strata bearing fossils such as trilobites and ammonites); continent-scale patterns of paleocurrents (for example, Chinle Formation)[17]; discontinuities in the stratigraphic record, such as paraconformities—gaps in the record with no apparent evidence for the amount of time supposedly represented; large scale volcanism (for example, Deccan basalts, India; Columbia River basalts, Northwestern U.S.)[18]; global/regional tectonic events (for example, mountain uplifting, plate movements, basin subsidence, massive sediment supply for basinal infilling)[19]; bolide impacts[20]—more than 150 structures of possible extraterrestrial impact origin since the Precambrian, some of which measure up to 250–300 kilometers in diameter (for example, Vredefort in South Africa, Chicxulub in Yucatan, Mexico).

Evidence 2: Fossil preservation and occurrence. The preservation of abundant organisms, their remains, or evidence of their activities (such as tracks and burrows) is very difficult to explain using present-day processes (that is, in actualistic terms), particularly when we consider the nature of the fossiliferous deposits. Many features of the fossils themselves support catastrophic events or rapid burial processes. A description of these features follows.

Abundance of mass mortality events throughout the record.[21] Currently, paleontologists recognize that the majority of these deposits formed catastrophically. An example of this is the massive burial of dinosaur remains. Thousands of bones and complete skeletons have been discovered. In many cases, sediments in which these remains are found contain a significant amount of volcanic material.

Worldwide extinction events.[22] Throughout the fossil record there are many (not only the popular "big five") strata that record the sudden disappearance of numerous taxa. For example, when discussing extinctions we usually refer to popular species like dinosaurs, trilobites,[23] and ammonites, but in reality there are hundreds of genera and many more species that not only have become extinct but most significantly have been preserved, something that is extremely uncommon in present day conditions.

Exquisite preservation of organisms.[24] Complete articulated skeletons have been found as well as preserved soft body parts (for example, whale's baleen; internal organs such as those in the Santana Formation fossilized fish; articulated shells in both clams and ostracodes [tiny shrimplike crustaceans]). These parts would have decayed rapidly had they been exposed for long on the surface (on land or under water). All point to rapid burial and/or rapid mineralization.

Opisthotonic posture of many well preserved articulated vertebrate skeletons. An extreme, dorsally hyperextended posture of the spine,[25] where the skull and neck are curved over the back, and strong extension of the tail, is attributed not to postmortem processes but rather "death throes," in turn the consequence of unusual chemical changes in the environment (for example, hypoxia, asphyxiation, environmental toxins), that could be reasonably expected in a catastrophic scenario.

Evidence 3: Appearance and distribution of fossil remains. Many types of data relating to the first occurrence of a fossil organism or group of organisms, and the subsequent distribution of those species in the record, support the biblical model well, and in turn present problems for an evolutionary interpretation.

The Cambrian explosion.[26] The sudden appearance of more than twenty phyla or different types of organisms poses a major problem for evolutionary theory, which proposes all forms of life came from a single common ancestor. With no real ancestors further down in the geologic record, the evidence supports a polyphyletic origin of life,[27] something one would expect in a model of creation including different "kinds." In fact, while evolutionary theory has proposed the development of life forms from a "universal common ancestor," the fossil biodiversity trend data in the fossil record depicts precisely the opposite—an "inverted tree of life." Several other sudden "explosions" present in the fossil record[28] suggest the existence of different lineages with separate origins. The diversity we see today may have come from diversification of the originally created kinds through a process of "descent with modification," to use darwinistic terminology. (In fact the biblical record is not incompatible with eventual evolutionary change such as microevolution and speciation.[29])

The sudden appearance of complex body plans and structures. An example of this is the classic complex optical nature of the trilobite compound eye, with no "simpler" eye structures found in the underlying strata.

The lack of intermediate forms between major phyla groups. Claimed "evolutionary links" turn out not to be such even for the paleontologists studying these fossils. In the last few years, several purported "evolutionary links" have been shown not to be such (for example, *Archaeopteryx* and the origin of birds).[30] The presence of these morphological gaps among higher taxonomic categories actually serves to document the lack of evolutionary continuity.

The occurrence of a number of successive strata containing allochthonous fossil remains (that is, remains that did not live there but were were transported into place) deposited catastrophically. The famous Yellowstone "petrified forests"[31] are an example where trees that first appeared to be in growth position turned out to have been transported from elsewhere.

Record of animal activity: The presence of "ichnofossils" (that is, trace fossils such as trackways and burrows, larval cases, and reptile and bird eggs).[32] This data is very valuable for the development of a depositional model since it means that throughout the formation of the fossil record some organisms remained alive and active. Even though this data implies that a certain length of time has elapsed, it also suggests that abundant sediment input is needed as well as rapid burial processes. In addition, the abundance of some of these remains (for example, thousands of dinosaur tracks and eggs in many different parts of the world), as well as the nature of the sediments in which they are preserved, suggest unusual, possibly stressed, environmental conditions that would correspond to a worldwide catastrophic scenario.

A survey of twenty-five reported fossil patterns and trends in the fossil record has been published, with an evaluation of them in relation to evolutionary and biblical accounts of earth history.[33] The study concluded that more research is needed, but, by comparing the Scriptures and the fossil record, a better understanding can be developed of the geologic column.

Conclusion

There is broad agreement among Christian earth scientists who trust the biblical account that the general aspect of the fossil record is catastrophic[34]—one of destruction and death. Much data in the fossil record points to dramatically different physical conditions existing in the past and does not support a naturalistic evolutionary history of life on earth. The sudden appearance of a diversity of complex life forms and the lack of morphological continuity affirms the biblical account of creation of many different kinds of organisms. Although there are still many questions, when the different types of data (that is, from geology and paleontology among others) are considered, there is significant evidence to support an interpretation of earth history that is consistent with the biblical record.

Roberto E. Biaggi *completed a science teaching degree in Argentina, an MS in biology at Walla Walla University, and one in geology at La Sierra University. He holds a PhD with emphasis in paleontology from Loma Linda University. He has taught natural sciences in Chile, Mexico, and Argentina. Various research projects have led to earth science publications and presentations at many scientific meetings. He currently teaches natural sciences and philosophy of science and religion at Universidad Adventista del Plata, where he also directs the South American Branch of the Geoscience Research Institute and contributes to the Institute's publication, Ciencia de los Orígenes.*

References

[1] See M. J. Benton, *The Fossil Record 2* (London: Chapman & Hall, 1993), 845; and the online database at http://www.fossilrecord.net/fossilrecord/index.html. Also see M. J. Benton, "Diversification and Extinction in the History of Life," *Science* 268 (1995): 52–58.

[2] A. Kalmar and D. J. Currie, "The Completeness of the Continental Fossil Record and Its Impact on Patterns of Diversification," *Paleobiology* 36, no. 1 (2010): 51–60.

[3] A "collector's curve" is a graph of the rate of discovery of new fossil types as more fossil specimens are collected. The line continues to rise as long as new types are discovered and then levels off when essentially all types have been found.

[4] See Dr. Raúl Esperante's chapter 14 on dinosaurs in this volume and his article in *Ministry* (December 2009), titled "What Does the Bible Say About Dinosaurs?" Available at http://www.ministrymagazine.org/archive/2009/December/what-does-the-bible-say-about-dinosaurs.

[5] For example, such as L. Brand with David Jarnes, *Beginnings: Are Science and Scripture Partners in the Search for Origins?* (Nampa, ID: Pacific Press®, 2006), 120, 121; Brand describes in his model 2, a "wholistic geology" model, in which the earth records geological processes that "have been operating from the time of the Fall [entrance of sin in the world] to the present."

[6] Recent literature by Adventist scientists who discuss many of the issues relating to earth history include L. Brand (2006); L. Brand, *Faith, Reason, and Earth History, A Paradigm of Earth and Biological Origins by Intelligent Design,* 2nd rev. ed. (Berrien Springs, MI: Andrews University Press, 2009); H. G. Coffin, R. H. Brown, and L. J. Gibson, *Origin by Design* (Hagerstown, MD: Review and Herald, 2005); R. M. Ritland, *A Search for Meaning in Nature: A New Look at Creation and Evolution* (Mountain View, CA: Pacific Press®, 1970); A. A. Roth, *Origins: Linking Science and Scripture* (Hagerstown, MD: Review and Herald, 1998); A. A. Roth, *Science Discovers God: Seven Convincing Lines of Evidence for His Existence* (Hagerstown, MD: Autumn House Publishing, 2008). Keep in mind that when we refer to the Biblical record (of creation week and the worldwide flood) we are referring to the traditional Seventh-day Adventist interpretation of the events recorded there. On the other hand the evolutionary view implies a materialistic atheistic explanation of history.

[7] Brand (2006), 120 (see endnote 4, also endnote 7).

[8] Brand (2006), 76 (see endnote 4).

[9] See V. R. Baker, "The Channeled Scabland: A Retrospective," *Annual Review of Earth and Planetary Science* 37 (2009): 393–411. In Baker's view, the stronghold of uniformitarianism on the geologic community has hindered the advancement of science. See also J. Soennichsen, *Bretz's Flood: The Remarkable Story of a Rebel Geologist and the World's Greatest Flood* (WA: Sasquatch Books, 2009), 289.

[10] D. Garcia-Castellanos et al., "Catastrophic Flood of the Mediterranean After the Messinian Salinity Crisis," *Nature* 462 (2009): 778–781.

[11] S. Gupta et al., "Catastrophic Flooding Origin of Shelf Valley Systems in the English Channel," *Nature* 448 (2007): 342–345.

[12] Brand (2006); Roth (1998); G. Shanmugam, "50 Years of the Turbidite Paradigm (1950s–1990s): Deep-Water Processes and Facies Models: A Critical Perspective," *Marine and Petroleum Geology* 17 (2000): 285–342.

[13] B. C. Yang et al., "Wave-Generated Tidal Bundles as an Indication of Wave-Dominated Tidal Flats," *Geology* 36 (2008): 39–42.

[14] See M. Brongersma-Sanders, "Mass Mortality in the Sea," *GSA Memoir* 67 (1957): 941–1010; M. Lockley and A. Rice, "Volcanism and Fossil Biotas," *GSA Special Paper* 244 (1990): 1–136.

[15] P. Schulte et al., "The Chicxulub Asteroid Impact and Mass Extinction at the Cretaceous-Paleogene Boundary," *Science* 327 (2010): 1214–1218. Read about the latest debate on the causes of the K-T mass extinction in *Science* 328 (2010): 973, 974; R. A. F. Grieve, "Terrestrial Impact Structures," *Annual Review of Earth and Planetary Science* 15 (1987): 245–270.

[16] Baker (2009); D. V. Ager, *The Nature of the Stratigraphical Record,* 3rd ed. (New York: John Wiley and Sons, 1993), 151.

[17] R. F. Dubiel et al., "The Pangaean Megamonsoon—Evidence From the Upper Triassic Chinle Formation, Colorado Plateau," *Palaios* 6 (1991): 347–370; Roth (1998).

[18] J. P. Lockwood and R. W. Hazlett, *Volcanoes: Global Perspectives* (NJ: John Wiley & Sons Ltd., 2010), 543.

[19] P. Kearey et al., *Global Tectonics,* 3rd ed. (NJ: Wiley-Blackwell, 2009), 499.

[20] K. R. Evans et al., eds., "The Sedimentary Record of Meteorite Impacts," *GSA Special Paper* 437 (2008).

[21] For an example, see D. M. Martill et al., "Mass Mortality of Fishes in the Santana Formation (Lower Cretaceous ?Albian) of Northeast Brazil," *Cretaceous Research* 29 (2008): 649–658; also D. J. Varricchio and J. R. Horner, "Hadrosaurid and Lambeosaurid Bone Beds From the Upper Cretaceous 2 Medicine Formation of Montana—Taphonomic and Biologic Implications," *Canadian Journal of Earth Sciences* 30, no. 5 (1993): 997–1006.

[22] C. Koeberl and K. G. MacLeod, eds., "Catastrophic Events and Mass Extinctions: Impacts and Beyond," *GSA Special Paper* 356 (2002).

[23] There are more than fifteen thousand species of trilobites, all of them extinct, to mention only one example.

[24] D. J. Bottjer et al., *Exceptional Fossil Preservation: A Unique View on the Evolution of Marine Life* (New York: Columbia University Press, 2002), 409; P. A. Allison, "Konservat-Lagerstätten: Cause and Classification," *Paleobiology* 14, no. 4 (1988): 331–344.

[25] C. M. Faux and K. Padian, "The Opisthotonic Posture of Vertebrate Skeletons: Postmortem Contraction or Death Throes?" *Paleobiology* 33, no. 2 (2007): 201–226.

[26] See A. A. Roth, *Science Discovers God* (2008), ch. 5. Roth points out the major problem of explaining the origin of nineteen different body plans in the phyla of the "Cambrian Explosion," when in the underlying Precambrian, and in very close stratigraphic proximity, there are only three.

[27] See Brand (2006), fig. 7.7 (A and B), for a description of the actual pattern found in the fossil record, in which the diversity of phyla (major category of organisms), contrary to what one would expect in an evolutionary model, is greater at the bottom of the record and decreases upwards in the geologic column.

[28] D. L. Rabosky and I. J. Lovette, "Explosive Evolutionary Radiations: Decreasing Speciation or Increasing Extinction Through Time?" *Evolution* 62 (2008): 1866–1875.

[29] For more on the question of microevolution and speciation within an interventionist (biblical) framework, see Brand (2006), 53.

[30] Roth, *Science Discovers God,* ch. 6, discusses at length this famous "intermediate" and all the controversy among the paleontologists studying the origin of birds, feathers, and flight.

[31] For more than a hundred years, scientists interpreted these successive layers as a succession of about forty-eight fossil forests. A body of data exists now (much of it as result of research stimulated by biblically shaped geohistorical paradigms) that suggests a catastrophic scenario of transported trees and vegetation such as the one documented after the eruption of Mount St. Helens. See W. J. Fritz, "Reinterpretation of the Depositional Environment of the Yellowstone 'Fossil Forests,'" *Geology* 8 (1980): 309–313. For a detailed discussion, see Coffin et al., *Origin by Design* (2005), ch. 18, and for a brief summary, Brand (2006), 156. These results might very well apply to other similar petrified forests.

[32] Brand (2006), 133–136, discusses the implications of trace fossils and fossil eggs in the fossil record. While many of these activities require time (and any model should account for it), the preservation of these remains indicates unusual and catastrophic conditions.

[33] See J. Gibson, "Fossil Patterns: A Classification and Evaluation," *Origins* 23, no. 2 (1996): 68–96. These reported patterns found in the fossil record are classified into four categories: fossil diversity patterns, fossil morphological patterns, fossil ecological patterns, and depositional patterns. Gibson concludes that from these patterns, catastrophic activity, global patterns, sudden, abrupt appearance of morphological disparity among marine animals in the "Cambrian Explosion," widespread extinction events, lack of ancestors in Precambrian rocks, and morphological gaps among higher taxa throughout the fossil record are all evidences expected within a biblical framework for the history of the earth.

[34] Almost twenty years ago, Ager (1993) suggested that "we are beginning to see a somewhat 'catastrophic' picture. It is evident that he has been proven right. In addition, this overall nature of the record might be directly related to the strong imprint of the taphonomic processes that led to the preservation of remains of organisms in the fossil record, what has been termed the 'taphonomic megabias' of the record." (Kalmar and Currie [2010], see endnote 2).

Chapter 13

How Do Plate Tectonics Relate to the Bible?

If someone asks you any question about geology and your answer includes the phrase "plate tectonics," you have a fairly good chance of being correct or at least on track to the right answer. Plate tectonic theory provides an explanation for the formation of volcanic and granitic rocks. It explains why mountains occur in some places and depressions in others; why the continents are above sea level and the ocean floor is below sea level. The theory also explains earthquakes as the sudden jerking of two plates slipping past each other.

To understand how plate tectonics relate to the Bible, this chapter first describes basic plate tectonic theory and the evidence for it. Geographic examples connect the theory to well-known earth features and demonstrate its all-encompassing applicability. Next, plate tectonic theory is related to the Bible by considering the history of the theory, Bible geography, and God's action in the world. Then plate tectonics issues are presented under the headings of scientific revolution, theodicy and catastrophe, time, pre-fossiliferous rocks, and heat dissipation.

The conclusion recognizes that much about plate tectonics is unknown because of our finite human understanding.

Plate tectonic theory

Plates and their movement. Plate tectonics involves more than just the splitting of a supercontinent (commonly referred to as Pangaea); it is the motion of all the continents and "subcontinents" in various changing directions. The earth is made up of seven major plates: six roughly equivalent to the six continents and the seventh encompassing much of the Pacific Ocean. Important smaller plates alluded to in this article include the Arabian, Indian, Philippine, and Caribbean Plates, and the Juan de Fuca, Cocos, and Nazca Plates along the east side of the Pacific Plate.

Most geologic activity of interest to researchers occurs at plate boundaries where two plates move apart (diverge), together (converge), or past each other (transform). At divergent spreading centers such as the inactive East African Rift and the active Mid-Atlantic Ridge, new crustal material is formed (for example, Surtsey, the volcanic island south of Iceland formed in 1963). At convergent subduction zones, mountains are formed, such as the Andes, Alps, Sierra Nevadas, and Himalayas, as are volcanic islands such as the Aleutians and Japan. At a transform boundary, two plates move past each other, such as at the San Andreas Fault in California and at the fault along the Jordan River Valley.

In addition to activity at plate boundaries, in some places hot magma from the earth's mantle ascends as a plume in plate interiors to heat the crust and produce volcanoes. Such a stationary hot spot under the moving Pacific Plate yielded the string of Hawaiian volcanoes, and another under North America produced volcanism across Idaho, culminating in present-day activity in Yellowstone.

Differentiation. According to theory, plate tectonic processes began in a homogeneous early earth. Magma welled up at early spreading centers, forming new oceanic crust. Volcanic and granitic rock was forged at subduction zones, making new continental crust. As material in the earth's interior partially melted, rose to the surface in magma form, and then crystallized, the earth's elements differentiated into lighter minerals at the surface and heavier ones in the interior. Several cycles of this process yielded the less dense mountains and continents above sea level and the denser ocean basins below sea level, since crustal rock of lower density "floats" higher on the earth's "liquid" interior.

Mechanisms. Three mechanisms have been suggested as causing plate tectonic motion: (1) plates are pushed apart as magma from the earth's mantle rises at the spreading centers to form new crust; (2) plates are pulled together as old crust is dragged back down into the mantle at subduction zones; and (3) crustal plates are carried along in "conveyor belt fashion" on top of convection cells that are in the plastic mantle of the earth's interior. The actual cause of plate tectonic motion is probably some combination of all three mechanisms.

Evidence. Evidence for plate tectonic theory comes from differing geochemical data in the earth's crust, mantle, and core, as well as from geophysical data (for example, seismic waves, heat flow rates, gravity variations, and the earth's magnetic field). Earthquakes provide the most direct evidence for plate motion. Less dramatic evidence comes from highly accurate GPS stations located on the various continents that indicate relative plate motions of 20–200 mm/year. Early evidence for plate motion came from maps showing similar contours of the Old World and New World continents, suggesting that they once fit together like a puzzle. In some locations, confirmation was provided by similar rocks and fossils located in matching regions of separated continents.

In the 1960s, ocean crust patterns provided compelling evidence leading to near-universal acceptance of plate tectonic theory. The radiometric ages and alternating magnetic patterns of the Atlantic Ocean floor seemed to be arranged symmetrically on both sides of the Mid-Atlantic Ridge. Plate tectonic theory provided a succinct explanation for this: oceanic crust was continuously formed as magma moved up, cooled and solidified, and then was pushed away from the spreading center in both directions. When the magma solidified, the iron-bearing minerals in it were frozen in alignment with the earth's magnetic field at the time. As the direction of the earth's magnetic field alternated between north and south, normal and reverse magnetic polarity directions were symmetrically frozen into the oceanic crust.

Plate tectonics and the Bible

Science from the Bible. Some early ideas related to plate tectonics were suggested by theologians. In 1668, French cleric François Placet suggested that "before the deluge America was not separated from the other parts of the earth." In the 1700s, German theologian Theodor Christoph Lilienthal suggested a separation of land by water based on an exegesis of 1 Chronicles 1:19 (or Genesis 11:25); however, if one associates plate tectonics with Noah's flood, the separation would have happened sooner than indicated in these verses. In 1858, French geographer Antonio Snider-Pellegrini noted the parallelism of opposing shores of the Atlantic Ocean and inferred that an originally continuous landmass had been split to form the Atlantic at the time of Noah's Flood.[1]

Bible geography. Important geographical features described in the Bible are the result of plate tectonic activity. Mount Sinai is made up of Precambrian granite emplaced before most fossils were buried. The island of Patmos is a recent volcanic formation, created as the African Plate subducted beneath the Eurasian Plate. Mount Hermon, the Sea of Galilee, the Jordan River, the Dead Sea, and the Gulf of Aqaba are located on a north-south transform fault where earthquakes frequently occur as the Arabian plate slips past the African plate. Parts of Galilee and the area east of the Dead Sea are covered with black volcanic basalt produced at the boundary between these two plates. These plates are pushed together at a bend in the transform fault to form Mount Hermon and are pulled apart in another place to form the Dead Sea depression. In the Red Sea, the plates are actually diverging at a spreading zone.

God's action. The Bible refers to plate tectonic activity when it describes earthquakes and volcanoes, and in some cases, the Scriptures indicate that these phenomena are directly caused by God. He apparently caused the earthquake that resulted in the swallowing up of Korah and company (Numbers 16:31, 32). Other earthquakes implying divine origin occurred during Jonathan's attack on the garrison in Gibeah (1 Samuel

14:15), while Elijah was at Horeb (1 Kings 19:11), at Jesus' crucifixion and resurrection (Matthew 27:51; 28:2), and when Paul was in prison at Philippi (Acts 16:26).

More indirectly, the Old Testament mentions an earthquake that occurred in the days of King Uzziah (Amos 1:1; Zechariah 14:5). Other references to the earth moving are more general (Job 9:6; Psalms 18:7; 46:2, 3; Jeremiah 4:24), are the result of judgment (Psalm 60:2; Isaiah 13:13, 14; 24:19, 20; 29:6), or are prophecies (Ezekiel 38:19; Zechariah 14:4; Matthew 24:7; Mark 13:8; Luke 21:11; Revelation 11:19).

Indications of God causing mountains to burn, melt, flow, or smoke may be references to volcanoes (Psalms 97:5; 144:5; Isaiah 34:9, 10; 64:1–3; Jeremiah 51:25). In the future, the elements will melt with fervent heat (2 Peter 3:10), and a lake of fire will be used in judgment (Revelation 19:20; 20:10, 14, 15; 21:8). When God descended upon Mount Sinai, it both quaked (Exodus 19:18; Psalms 68:8; 77:18; 114:4–7; Hebrews 12:26) and burned (Deuteronomy 4:11; 5:23; Judges 5:5). Other texts refer to both earthquake and volcanic type activity occurring at God's presence (Psalm 104:32; Micah 1:4; Nahum 1:5, 6).

Issues in plate tectonics

A scientific revolution. Plate tectonics provides a classic example of a scientific revolution—a major change in paradigm as new data becomes available. Alfred Wegener's ideas about continental drift in the 1920s were derided because he provided no mechanism for the continents to drift through the ocean floor like a ship plowing through an ice pack. Not until the 1960s were his ideas resurrected, albeit in a slightly different form, based on new data from the ocean floor. Now most every explanation in geology is connected in some way to the paradigm of plate tectonics. The new plate tectonic model incorporated much from previous geology theory, but the data are now set in a new framework. This exemplifies how an earth history model has changed in major ways and indicates that significant changes will no doubt occur in the years to come.

Theodicy and catastrophe. The Bible recognizes the cyclical uniformity of natural law (Ecclesiastes 1:4–7) but also warns of catastrophes. The 8.7 magnitude Lisbon earthquake of November 1755 was due to African Plate subduction beneath the Eurasian Plate. It triggered a five to ten meter high tsunami and killed 60,000 people. This led to questions about God's responsibility for evil, exemplified by Voltaire's book, *Candide.* The 9.1 magnitude Banda Aceh earthquake and resulting tsunami of December 2004 due to subduction of the Australian Plate beneath the Eurasian Plate killed more than 150,000 people. More recent examples are the 7.0 magnitude Haiti earthquake of January 2010 (from the Caribbean Plate moving past the North American plate) and the 8.8 magnitude Chilean earthquake of February 2010 (from the Nazca Plate subducting under the South American Plate). Examples of volcanic catastrophes include the destruction of Pompeii by Vesuvius (at the boundary between African and Eurasian Plates) and the 1980 eruption of Mount St. Helens (from the Juan de Fuca Plate subducting beneath the North American Plate).

Time. At the current rate of about twenty-five millimeters per year, the separation of the Old World and New World to their present positions would take about two hundred million years. To model rates of plate motion, in the 1980s, John Baumgardner used a Cray supercomputer at the Los Alamos National Laboratory in New Mexico, U.S.A. to write a Fortran computer program called Terra. Results from using standard parameters in the equations for his model have been reported in the scientific literature.[2] Baumgardner also used significantly different parameters to develop a catastrophic plate tectonic (CPT) model in collaboration with others.[3]

The CPT model begins with the breakup of a single supercontinent, Pangaea. The edges of Pangaea then sink into the mantle at ever faster rates due to a mutually accelerating increase in heating and weakening of the mantle. This runaway subduction induces rapid reversals of the earth's magnetic field, causes volcanic fissure eruptions, jettisons steam into the atmosphere that results in global rain, and raises the ocean floor displacing water onto the continents. The CPT model has been reported in *U.S. News & World Report*, with the summative statement, "Indeed, there is universal agreement that Terra, created to prove the Bible literally true, is one of the most useful and powerful geological tools in existence."[4]

It must be noted that this CPT model has several scientific difficulties. First, postulating rapid reversals in the whole earth's magnetic field is problematic. Evidence is available for some rapid local changes in magnetic field,[5] but explanations for rapid global changes remain hypothetical.[6]

Pre-fossiliferous rocks. The second problem with the CPT model is that it begins with the unidirectional rifting of Pangaea in the middle of the fossiliferous (fossil-containing) Phanerozoic part of the geologic column. The model does not address the evidence for multidirectional plate motion in the early Phanerozoic part of the geologic record, nor in the even earlier nonfossiliferous Precambrian part. The evidence suggests that the plates moved back and forth in what are termed "Wilson cycles" rather than in just one direction,[7] and that most of the continental land masses were formed by plate tectonic activity during the Precambrian.

Heat. Third, for the plates to move nine orders of magnitude faster (that is, in two months instead of two hundred million years), the mantle viscosity (resistance to flow) must be a billion times smaller than at present. Since viscosity varies exponentially with temperature, this decreased viscosity would be possible only if the mantle temperature were hundreds of degrees greater than at present; however, the higher temperatures would be expected to yield different types of rocks.

Fourth, and perhaps most problematic, heat from all the magma must be dissipated quickly—again, about a billion times faster than at present. This difficulty has been noted from the standard scientific perspective,[8] as well as by Baumgardner himself.[9] His response is, "The Flood catastrophe cannot be understood or modeled in terms of time-invariant laws of nature. Intervention by God in the natural order during and after the catastrophe appears to be a logical necessity. Manifestations of the intervention appear to include . . . a loss of thermal energy afterward."

Conclusion

The pros and cons of the CPT model have been debated in the creationist literature by Baumgardner and Oard.[10] Walter Brown has hypothesized an alternative theory, which suggests that the pre-Flood earth's crust was ruptured by the considerable amount of water under it. The escaping water covered the earth and the broken pieces of crust formed hydroplates that rapidly slid to the location of what are now the continents.[11] Sam Carey's much older expanding-earth model has also been analyzed for its merits and problems.[12] My conclusion is that plate tectonic theory seems to be well-founded, but the science does not fit easily with a recent one-year flood.

As is the case in many other areas of human investigation, when we study origins issues, we must trust the details to an all-wise God, since His "foolishness" is greater than our wisdom (1 Corinthians 1:25ff). God has a thousand means at his disposal to bring about things of which we know nothing—with God all things are possible (Matthew 19:26; Luke 18:27). Scientists can continue to ask questions but, like Job, must continue to fully trust God in the process (see Job 13:15).

Ben Clausen *received an MS in geology from Loma Linda University and a PhD in physics from the University of Colorado. His nuclear physics research at a number of particle accelerators and the University of Virginia resulted in several dozen publications. Current plate tectonic research on Southern California granitic rocks has been presented at geology conferences in the United States, South Africa, Norway, and India. Since 1990 he has studied science and religion issues at the Geoscience Research Institute and has lectured worldwide. For many years he organized the Seventh-day Adventist Church's science and religion meetings and in 2006 co-authored a book on origins.*

References

[1] J. Romm, "A New Forerunner for Continental Drift," *Nature* 367 (1994): 407, 408.

[2] H. P. Bunge et al., "Time Scales and Heterogeneous Structure in Geodynamic Earth Models," *Science* 280 (1998): 91–95.

[3] S. Austin et al., "Catastrophic Plate Tectonics: A Global Flood Model of Earth History," in *Proceedings of the Third International Conference on Creationism,* R. Walsh, ed. (Pittsburgh, PA: Creation Science Fellowship, 1994), 609–621, *Putting the Puzzle Pieces Together: Global Tectonics and the Flood* (Answers in Genesis, 2006) DVD.

[4] C. Burr, "The Geophysics of God: A Scientist Embraces Plate Tectonics—and Noah's Flood," *U. S. News & World Report* 122, no. 23 (1997): 55–58.

[5] R. Coe, M. Prévot, and P. Camps, "New Evidence for Extraordinarily Rapid Change of the Geomagnetic Field During a Reversal," *Nature* 374 (1995): 687–692.

[6] D. Humphreys, "Physical Mechanism for Reversals of the Earth's Magnetic Field During the Flood," in *Proceedings of the Second International Conference on Creationism,* R. Walsh and C. Brooks, eds. (Pittsburgh, PA: Creation Science Fellowship, 1990): 129–142.

[7] Austin et al. (1994).

[8] R. Barnes, "Thermal Consequences of a Short Time Scale for Sea-Floor Spreading," *Journal of the American Scientific Affiliation* 32, no. 2 (1980): 123–125.

[9] J. Baumgardner, "Numerical Simulation of the Large-Scale Tectonic Changes Accompanying the Flood," in *Proceedings of the First International Conference on Creationism,* R. Walsh, C. Brooks, and R. Crowell, eds. (Pittsburgh, PA: Creation Science Fellowship, 1986), 17–30.

[10] J. Baumgardner and M. Oard, "Forum on Catastrophic Plate Tectonics," *Technical Journal* 16, no. 1 (2002): 57–85.

[11] W. Brown Jr., *In the Beginning: Compelling Evidence for Creation and the Flood* (Phoenix, AZ: Center for Scientific Creation, 2001).

[12] B. Mundy, "Expanding Earth?" *Origins* 15, no. 2 (1988): 53–69.

Chapter 14

How Do Dinosaurs Fit in a Biblical Perspective?

If you've ever visited a natural history museum, you've probably seen spectacular, massive dinosaur skeletons. TV documentaries also show us lifelike, animated dinosaur re-creations. Paleontologists have found evidence of dinosaurs in sediments on every continent, even in Antarctica, including bones, eggs, nests, and footprints. Especially abundant are dinosaur footprints and trackways, found by the thousands in the U.S., Argentina, Spain, France, Russia, China, Mongolia, and northern Africa, to name a few of the more prominent locations. It seems that dinosaurs existed on earth for a limited period of time. In some places, they appear to have been numerous, based on the number of bones and/or footprints we have found.

Learning about dinosaurs

The study of dinosaur bones, eggs, and footprints has provided valuable information about their size, physiology, likely social behavior, and probable habitats; however, a degree of uncertainty exists due to the interpretive nature of evidence. Although some dinosaurs were the largest terrestrial animals to ever live, others were actually small—the size of a sheep or a dog. For instance, *Struthiomimus* was the size of a contemporary ostrich, and *Compsognathus* was no bigger than the rooster of today. Dinosaurs were well adapted to their habitats, which included rivers, lakeshores, beaches, forests, swamps, deserts, and plains.

It's important to be aware of a few things about the skeletons in museum displays. First, what we see are typically not the actual bones, but replicas. The original bones are too valuable and delicate for display; they're usually stored safely within the museum. In addition, the "complete" display skeletons are assembled from replicas of bones coming from more than one specimen. On occasion, these specimens are found in locations quite distant from each other. Nonetheless, the museum replicas are reasonably trustworthy. Some complete specimens have been unearthed, including the *Tyrannosaurus rex* exhibited in the Chicago Field Museum. The animations seen on television, however, are much more speculative, especially regarding skin color, physiology, and behavior.

According to the evolutionary viewpoint, dinosaurs originated from other animal ancestors through the gradual processes of mutation and natural selection. Their remains in the geologic column appear in rock layers that paleontologists label Triassic, Jurassic, and Cretaceous, which according to the geologic time scale, spanned 250 to 65 million years ago. Some paleontologists believe dinosaurs and other groups of plants and animals disappeared suddenly due to a gigantic meteorite impact at the close of the Cretaceous period, some sixty-five million years ago. Others doubt this model, pointing to its inconsistencies.[1]

The disappearance of dinosaurs isn't the only abrupt occurrence in the fossil record; they also make a sudden appearance. In other words, their fossils show up without any known ancestor or predecessor.[2] This is not what we would expect in the gradual evolution model, where different forms and groups of plants and animals allegedly evolved from less complex ancestors. In other words, if macroevolution were true, then we would expect to see the gradual appearance of dinosaurs in the record of fossils. Instead, we find the opposite—the appearance of fully formed, diversified dinosaurs, demonstrating adaptation to their habitat.

A disappearing act

Dinosaurs vanished from the fossil record worldwide at the topmost layer of Cretaceous rock. A few paleontologists assert that birds are the descendants of dinosaurs. They base their conclusion on disputed feather impressions found on some fossil dinosaurs, as well as on bone features typical of birds that are found in other dinosaur fossils. This controversial notion, based on a limited understanding of intermediate characteristics, fails to convincingly establish a dinosaur-bird lineage and doesn't explain the lack of extant dinosaurs to date.

As mentioned above, most evolutionary scientists claim that dinosaur extinction resulted from a huge meteorite impact at the end of the Cretaceous period. Such an impact would have released large amounts of dust and debris into the atmosphere, blocking the sun and causing a global cooling of the earth. Additionally, fires triggered by the heat of the impact would have consumed many large forests around the planet, and dust and ash would have increased the toxicity of the air and water. The combination of cool temperatures and high environmental toxicity might have triggered massive die-offs of dinosaurs and other organisms.

However, this model faces tremendous scientific challenges. The sedimentary record of the Cretaceous layer and the rocks above it show no global extinction of fish (including sharks), nor of turtles, salamanders, frogs, and various groups of marine invertebrate organisms and plants.[3] How could dinosaurs go globally extinct and other groups of animals not? Frogs, salamanders, turtles and many plants are very sensitive to alteration in climate. It seems unlikely they would have survived a radically changed, post-impact climate on a global scale.

Dinosaurs and the Flood

The long-age, evolutionary model faces many problems in explaining both the origin and disappearance of dinosaurs. Is it possible to study dinosaurs (and other fossils) in a way that is consistent with the biblical model of creation? How do we interpret dinosaurs in a recent-Creation, global-flood framework? Were dinosaurs the result of millions of years of animal evolution, or were they God's creation? These are important questions for the Bible believer because Scripture affirms that God created the animal kingdom and that He declared His Creation to be good. How do dinosaurs fit in this picture?

Most creationist scientists believe that dinosaurs disappeared, together with many other species, during the worldwide Flood, as described in Genesis 7:22. This scenario might also include meteorite activity, resulting in gigantic tsunamis, volcanic activity, and emission of carbon dioxide, sulphides, and other chemicals harmful to plants and animals. Therefore, the idea of one or more meteorites impacting the earth is not incompatible with the biblical model of the Flood.

-6

In spite of a lack of consensus among scientists about what made dinosaurs disappear, the popular media as well as some scientists have decided that the meteor impact theory is the only valid explanation. However, this is far from reality. Dinosaurs did disappear, but we don't know precisely when or why. Their extinction during the Genesis flood (with or without an associated impact) is a plausible hypothesis, deserving our consideration. In fact, some evidence is consistent with this hypothesis. Often, dinosaur remains are found in massive burials consisting of tens to thousands of individuals, including young and adults buried together. Examples of these dinosaur graveyards occur in the western U.S. (Colorado, Utah, Wyoming), Canada, Spain, China, Mongolia, and other places. Scientists have explained some of these massive occurrences as the result of a local catastrophe (for example, a mudslide, local flood, dune collapse),[4] but they could instead be explained as the result of local geologic activity during a worldwide flood, such as the one described in Genesis.

Do dinosaurs make sense in a biblical Creation?

The study of both the origin and extinction of dinosaurs can be approached within a biblical worldview framework. The book of Genesis says that on the sixth day of Creation week, God created "livestock, creatures that move along the ground, and wild animals, each according to its kind" (1:24, NIV). This group of creatures might well have included dinosaurs. "And to all the beasts of the earth and all the birds of the air and all the creatures that move on the ground—everything that has the breath of life in it—I give every green plant for food," stated God (Genesis 1:30). But, where do carnivorous dinosaurs fit in this perfect, all-vegetarian world? The biblical account (Genesis 3:14–19) suggests that the divine curse following Adam and Eve's Fall triggered some biological (that is, genetic) modifications that originated changes in the diet of some animals, and brought about competition, predation, disease, and perhaps parasitism, most likely over the span of several generations. Is this possible? Recent research in genetics has shown how major physiological and even anatomical changes can occur by a slight modification in the activity of regulatory genes.[5]

Dinosaurs and human beings

Much has been written and argued regarding evidence that supposedly shows dinosaur and human coexistence. The evidence includes what are interpreted to be human footsteps together with dinosaur footprints, as well as prehistoric pictures in caves and on pottery, where human figures appear with exceptional creatures very similar to current reconstructions of these giant reptiles. However, rigorous scientific study by creationist scientists has shown that these features have been misinterpreted.

Let us analyze, for example, the alleged "human" and dinosaur prints found in the riverbed of the Paluxy River, in Texas. A few decades ago, some enthusiastic scientists proclaimed this constituted evidence proving the existence of a worldwide flood. Intrigued by these statements, more than one evolutionist and creationist scientist studied in detail the marks found on the rocks. Laboratory studies were carried out by creationist scientists. An authentic print should present a deformation in the sediment under the print, which is normally left as a result of the animal's weight. To test for this characteristic deformation, scientists cut the print crosswise and observed no such deformation was present. They concluded that the shape was not a real human footprint, but instead a *pseudoprint* resulting from erosion.[6] Some people believe that certain "prints" and drawings probably had been fabricated to appear human-like. Uncritical use of poorly supported arguments harms true research being conducted by creationist scientists. Most of these researchers have learned to be more careful and accurate in their statements.

Dinosaurs and the Bible

The story of Creation in Genesis 1 tells of a God who created sea life as well as birds on the fifth day and the rest of the animals on the sixth day. Although reptiles are included among the animals created, dinosaurs are not specifically mentioned. Moses, who authored the book of Genesis, would not have had a specific word to refer to the dinosaur, nor was it necessary for him to mention them specifically in his narrative—after all, he didn't mention many other groups of animals (for example, beetles, sharks, or starfish) that God created. Some find dinosaurs too strange or ugly to be a part of God's Creation. Currently, there are many animals just as strange in appearance as dinosaurs that don't draw that much attention. Others believe that dinosaurs appeared as the result of the curse after Adam and Eve's sin, but the Bible does not identify which animals changed as a result of sin or what kind of changes might have occurred.

Most creationist scientists believe dinosaurs disappeared during or shortly after the Genesis flood; however, the Bible does not specify the fate of these animals. The idea that dinosaurs disappeared during the worldwide catastrophe we call the Flood is a hypothesis we should seriously consider, but only through scientific research, since the Bible is silent on the matter. The demonstration of this hypothesis should come from geological and paleontological data, but not from reading our ideas into the Bible.

Some creationists have suggested that dinosaurs might have been preserved in the ark, survived the Flood, and disappeared shortly after, while unsuccessfully attempting to adjust to a greatly changed environment. This is also a possibility, since perhaps some dinosaurs were inside the ark and afterwards disappeared during the postdiluvian colonization. The Bible mentions two strange creatures, Behemoth (Job 40:15–18) and Leviathan (Job 41:1), which some interpret as possible examples of postdiluvian dinosaurs. However, most Bible scholars do not accept this explanation, and the words *Behemoth* and *Leviathan* are usually translated as hippopotamus and crocodile, respectively.

Conclusion

Scripture does not mention the existence of dinosaurs—at least not as we now identify them—neither before nor after the Genesis Flood. Of course, the fact that the Bible doesn't mention dinosaurs doesn't constitute evidence that they never existed. It is simply another topic, among others, about which the Bible says nothing, providing us with fascinating questions to pursue.

The physical evidence pointing to their existence is clear. We have found dinosaur bones, teeth, eggs, footprints, and even impressions of their skin. At some point in history they disappeared. Their extinction may have taken place before, during, or even after the Genesis Flood.

Like the rest of the fossils, the origin and disappearance of dinosaurs are wrapped in mystery. However, dinosaurs do not challenge or compromise our faith in the Bible's teachings. They require careful and rigorous study, something Christians with the interest and talent should be strongly encouraged to do.

Raúl Esperante obtained a bachelor's degree in biology in his homeland, Spain, where he also worked as a science teacher in a secondary school. He then moved to the United States, where he completed a PhD in paleontology at Loma Linda University. Currently he works as a paleontologist for the Geoscience Research Institute in California. His interests include the study of fossilization processes, paleoecology, paleoenvironments, and issues related to science and faith. He has written several scholarly articles for peer-review scientific journals and participated in scientific congresses in many countries.

References

[1] For a detailed and extensive discussion, see the debate held online at the Geological Society of London: http://www.geolsoc.org.uk/gsl/views/debates/chicxulub.

[2] The best paleontologists do is to speculate about which reptile group dinosaurs evolve from. See M. J. Benton, "Origin and Early Evolution of Dinosaurs," in *The Complete Dinosaur*, J. O. Farlow and M. K. Brett-Surman, eds. (Bloomington, IN: Indiana University Press, 1997), 204–215.

[3] D. A. Russell and P. Dodson, "The Extinction of the Dinosaurs: A Dialogue Between a Catastrophist and a Gradualist," in *The Complete Dinosaur*, J. O. Farlow and M. K. Brett-Surman, eds. (Bloomington, IN: Indiana University Press, 2007), 662–672.

[4] M. J. Benton et al., *The Age of Dinosaurs in Russia and Mongolia* (Cambridge: Cambridge University Press, 2000), 289–292; J. G. Scotchmoor et al., *Dinosaurs: The Science Behind the Stories* (Alexandria, VA: American Geological Institute, 2002), 192; A. Martin, *Introduction to the Study of Dinosaurs* (Oxford: Blackwell, 2006), 206, 207.

[5] M. C. King and A. C. Wilson, "Evolution at Two Levels in Humans and Chimpanzees," *Science* 188 (1975): 107–116; S. B. Carroll, "Evolution at Two Levels: On Genes and Form," PLOS *Biology* 3 (2005): 1159–1166.

[6] A. V. Chadwick, "Of Dinosaurs and Men," *Origins* 14 (1987): 33–40.

Chapter 15

Does the Theory of Evolution Explain the Diversity of Life?

The answer you may receive to the question posed above will differ greatly depending on who you ask. Evolutionary theory is a vast and far-reaching body of ideas, buttressed by huge amounts of careful scholarship, and offers immense explanatory power. For most biologists, Theodosius Dobzhansky's statement[1] that "nothing in biology makes sense except in the light of evolution" is literally true. Though most biologists do not study evolution directly, they work within a framework of ideas that supposes all living organisms are united by common descent. Because they assume common descent to be true, they work as if it were so. However, a minority of biologists, ourselves included, perceive some major gaps in the evolutionary paradigm, which in our view call into question its ability to explain the full diversity of life.

Evolution depicts the diverse assemblage of living things via an "evolutionary tree" (figure 1), which postulates all species are united by a branching pattern of descent from a common ancestor. This ancestor, thought to have formed spontaneously from nonliving materials, forms the root of the tree. Various lines of its descendants form the different branches, all the way out to the twigs (not shown) that represent species—living or fossil. Each major evolutionary change or innovation is represented by a new branch on the tree. The whole tree is held together by its roots and major branching points. Those points will be the focus of this essay.

The root of the tree

A whole set of significant gaps in explanatory power can be found at the tree's base—in abiogenesis, or the forming of life from nonliving materials.[2] The first postulated step in abiogenesis is the production of simple organic molecules (for example, amino acids) from inorganic materials. Although these molecules have been synthesized, the conditions required are not plausible on an early earth. The next step is polymerization—the linking of the small molecules together. While a few natural conditions allowing polymerization have been found, none help form the precise, complicated sequences characteristic of molecules in living cells. The gap between what random polymerization processes can be shown to produce and the simplest living cell is enormous.

Another feature characterizing living things is the ability to reproduce detailed copies of themselves, which in turn are also able to reproduce. This highly complex process involves a whole suite of different molecules, all interacting with one another in a precisely directed way. However, the entire complicated system of molecules is required in order for the cell to be able to copy itself. If any part of the chain of interacting molecules is missing, the entire process fails and the cell cannot function or reproduce itself. This fact has long been recognized as a formidable challenge for the evolutionary theory of the origin of life.[3]

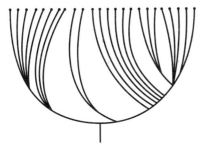

Figure 1. An evolutionary tree. The branches represent higher taxa such as phyla.

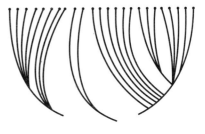

Figure 2. Evolutionary tree with hypothetical last common ancestors removed.

Looking beyond the molecules themselves to the organized structure of the cell, we see that living things are extremely complex, ordered systems with specific architecture. Many cellular components are essentially molecular machines, with interacting parts functioning in ways similar to human-designed machines.[4] Just as the structure of an automobile is not inherent in the basic properties of metal, plastic, and paint, neither is the structure of living cells inherent in the properties of the molecules of which they are made. Instead, cells are "built" in specific ways with the complicated patterns and combinations of materials required to carry out their functions.

The cell must constantly work to maintain its internal environment and keep itself in a functional state. The DNA (an acid containing the instructions necessary for the functioning of all living organisms) stores detailed information for how this is done, and how all cell functions are carried out. However, such information is not inherent in the structure of DNA either. Much as the sentiments expressed in a sonnet do not arise spontaneously from properties of the alphabet, the cell's information had to be put there by some means outside of what can be found in the properties of DNA itself. The lack of a naturalistic source for this information represents another important gap in the theory of abiogenesis. Thus, the lack of a credible explanation for life's origin leaves evolutionary theory with no known root for the evolutionary tree (see figure 2).

The major branches of the tree

We will next explore the attachment of major branches to the evolutionary tree. While evolutionary models attempt to explain how evolutionary information can arise incrementally by a combination of random mutation and natural selection, these models work best for rearranging information that is already present, such as may occur with species changing gradually over time. This is analogous to variations along the branches of the evolutionary tree.

The models quickly encounter huge and growing probability problems when attempting to explain how random changes could have produced large amounts of the new, specific, and complex information needed for originating life or producing an inherently new and different kind of creature.[5] However, this is precisely what would be needed to produce a new branch on the tree. Attempts at an explanation have been made, such as exaptation (using existing parts for a new and different purpose than their original function).[6] However, these explanations do not reveal how the original function developed in the first place, or what directs the parts to come together in a new way to perform some other function. No doubt much more research will be done on this question in the future.

Another hurdle for explaining the diversity of life via the evolutionary model is based on the structure of chromosomes. Chromosomes are composed of DNA, a very long, linear molecule. Genes, which contain the information necessary for cell function, are sequences lined up like sentences along the DNA strands. Occasionally, a gene is accidentally duplicated, producing an extra copy. The mutation/selection model of evolution posits that random small changes (mutations) in the DNA of the extra gene copy slowly accumulate. If these differences provide a benefit, they will be favored by natural selection. Over time, the model suggests that these small changes can produce a gene that performs a new function radically different from the original one.

One problem with this model stems from the fact that most mutations either have little effect or are in fact harmful. These harmful or slightly harmful mutations are likely to be much more common than any rare, beneficial mutation. Some evolutionists have presented mathematical models purporting to show how beneficial mutations can accrue by selection and eventually form new genes. Yet these models rarely account for the fact that each beneficial mutation will be linked to a large number of harmful or meaningless mutations since they are all part of the same long chain of DNA. Given accepted estimates of ratios of beneficial to harmful mutations, models that take this into account suggest that the rare beneficial mutations will be swamped by the cumulative effect of the many harmful mutations linked to them on the DNA.[7]

These harmful mutations may be in the same gene or in more distant genes that are nevertheless linked by being on the same chromosome, all of which is usually inherited as a unit. In other words, it is difficult to take many steps forward while you are strongly tied to many other individuals that are taking steps backward. It is true that this linkage is not absolute—genes do have ways of swapping positions and rearranging on the chromosome. Nevertheless, the principle of negative mutations outnumbering positive ones should be true regardless of what portion of the chromosome a gene is in. At the very least, this gene linkage greatly complicates the already formidable barrier to producing genes for new, functional molecules by purely random mutation and natural selection. This linkage issue would be a problem for virtually any new evolutionary feature and would likely apply to many of both small and large branches on the evolutionary tree.

Artificial selection is another line of evidence providing insights into the problems of producing new branches on the evolutionary tree. Darwin used the analogy of artificial selection to claim that natural selection could accomplish even larger-scale changes given enough time. But many scientists are skeptical that the small-scale changes observed in breeding experiments, or in nature, are sufficient to explain the differences among major groups of organisms. Can nature produce a horse from a fish using the same kinds of changes we observe from our study of finch beaks or our experience in breeding dogs or chickens? Probably not, irrespective of the amount of time available.[8] The problem lies in the need for *new* genetic information, not merely an increase or decrease in the information that already exists. We can see how a single ancestral species may produce a variety of descendant species adapted to different environments, but the resulting pattern looks more like one small tree in a forest of separate trees than a single tree (figure 3).

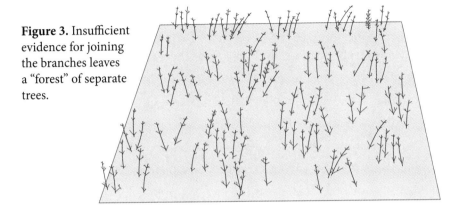

Figure 3. Insufficient evidence for joining the branches leaves a "forest" of separate trees.

Fossils and the evolutionary tree

The fossil record provides another way of assessing the problems of evolutionary branching. One of the most striking features of the fossil record is the abrupt appearance of most phyla (major types of organisms) in a relatively short stratigraphic interval in the Cambrian rock layers. This pattern, known as the Cambrian Explosion, offers one of the most compelling lines of evidence against the evolutionary tree. A large number of phyla and classes of animals found in the Cambrian have no ancestors or links to each other. The pattern is well summarized by the phrase "disparity precedes diversity."[9] In other words, the major differences among living organisms appear earlier in the fossil record than the many varieties with minor differences. No fossil evidence exists showing a gradual divergence over long ages to produce organisms with new body plans.[10]

Systematic gaps are another feature of the fossil record that does not support evolutionary theory.[11] The shortage of transitional fossils is a widely recognized feature of the fossil record, expressed in the familiar phrase "missing link." Occasionally one hears reports of the discovery of a previously missing fossil link, and these discoveries are hailed as evidence of evolutionary connections between different branches of the evolutionary tree. However, the most significant aspect of the problem is that the links are missing in a particular pattern.

We may compare the fossil record of horses and donkeys, for example, with that of clams and crabs. Horses and donkeys are very similar, and one might easily explain a lack of intermediates between them. After all, there might be only two or three intermediate species and therefore little chance of finding a fossil from such a small sample. In contrast, clams and crabs are very different. Following evolutionary theory, the number of fossil links connecting them to a common ancestor should thus number in the thousands. One would logically expect to find many fossils from such a large sample. In fact, the reality is exactly the opposite. There are many species of fossil horses, some of which may be regarded as linking horses and donkeys, while there are virtually no fossils that are believed to link clams and crabs. This is exactly the pattern one would expect if different types of organisms originated independently and varied within limits. Again, the pattern is more like a forest of independent trees than like a single evolutionary tree.

A few examples of evolutionary links between higher taxa (or families of organisms) have been proposed, some of which appear quite convincing at first glance. When examined critically, they are not compelling to those with doubts about evolution. One important problem is the sequence in which some of these species appear in the fossil record. The fish-tetrapod fossils provide a good example. Soon after

Darwin's theory was published, scientists began looking for potential evolutionary ancestors for the terrestrial vertebrates.[12] Lungfish were the first ancestors proposed, but were deemed too specialized. In the 1940s, the fossil fish *Eusthenopteron* was described in detail and became the model of a tetrapod ancestor. Description of the fossil fish *Panderichthys* in 1980, and *Tiktaalik*[13] in 2006 provided further examples of fossils with combinations of traits intermediate between fish and tetrapods. This fossil sequence has been used to argue to show that tetrapods evolved from the lobe-finned fish. More recently, however, a fossil tetrapod trackway was found in a layer lower in the strata than the fossil fish purported to be the tetrapod ancestor.[14] In evolutionary terms, the purported descendant came before its ancestor—obviously impossible. Thus, it seems some other factor(s) must be at work in producing this fossil sequence.

Fossil whales provide another example of a proposed evolutionary series. Several fossil mammals have been found that are claimed to be whale ancestors.[15] These fossils show combinations of traits unlike anything living today, and seem to show a trend of increasing similarity to whales. However, none of these fossil species is believed to be ancestral to any other known species, living or fossil. If one wishes to determine whether these fossils were part of an evolutionary lineage or were separately created, one must consult some explanatory theory, since the evidence is quite incomplete. An evolutionist could accept them as the result of evolution, while a creationist can look for another explanation, such as separately created kinds, or as the result of some unknown factor such as is illustrated in the tetrapod example in the previous paragraph.

Summary

In summary, although most scientists would say that evolution is adequate to explain the diversity of life, in our view it falls far short of that goal for several reasons. These include the lack of an information source for new forms, linked harmful mutations swamping beneficial ones, fossil disparity before diversity, and systematic gaps in the fossil record. Collectively, these observations show that the evolutionary tree is imaginary, and that the pattern of nature is more accurately illustrated by a "forest" of trees that represent independently created lineages. We believe that evolution cannot explain the origin of life, the origin of any major new form, or even the development of major new structures within an existing form. Therefore, it cannot explain the broad diversity of life we see today. To us, the evidence inherent in the structure of life itself is compelling evidence that "in the beginning, God created" a diversity of "kinds."

David L. Cowles is a native of the Pacific Northwest and has loved biology all his life. After an MS in biology from Walla Walla College and two years of teaching academy science, he moved to California for a PhD at the University of California, Santa Barbara, where he studied metabolism of deep-sea species. Upon graduation, he joined Loma Linda University, where he taught for fourteen years before moving to Walla Walla University in 2001. He is still in love with biology, whether teaching, conducting research, or mentoring graduate students. He can be found at the Rosario Beach Marine Station doing research and teaching classes almost every summer.

*(The biography of **L. James Gibson** can be found on page 33.)*

References

¹ T. Dobzhansky, "Nothing in Biology Makes Sense Except in the Light of Evolution," *American Biology Teacher* 35 (1973): 125–129.

² For more detailed discussion on the problems in abiogenesis, see chapter 9 by Javor in this volume.

³ S. C. Meyer, *Signature in the Cell: DNA and the Evidence for Intelligent Design* (New York: HarperCollins Publishers, 2009).

⁴ M. J. Behe, *Darwin's Black Box* (New York: Free Press, 1996).

⁵ M. J. Behe, *The Edge of Evolution* (New York: Free Press, 2007), 320; D. L. Overman, *A Case Against Accident and Self-Organization* (Lanhan, MD: Rowman and Littlefield Publishers, 1997), 244.

⁶ First proposed by S. J. Gould and E. S. Vrba, "Exaptation—A Missing Term in the Science of Form," *Paleobiology* 8 (1982): 4–15.

⁷ J. C. Sanford, *Genetic Entropy and the Mystery of the Genome* (Waterloo, NY: FMS Publications, 2008), 232; the effect is known as "Muller's Ratchet."

⁸ J. Valentine and D. Erwin, "Interpreting Great Developmental Experiments: The Fossil Record," in *Development as an Evolutionary Process*, R. A. Raff and E. C. Raff, eds. (New York: Alan R. Liss, Inc., 1985), 95, 96.

⁹ See S. J. Gould, *Wonderful Life: The Burgess Shale and the Nature of History* (NY: Norton, 1989), 49.

¹⁰ D. Erwin, J. Valentine, and J. Sepkoski, "A Comparative Study of Diversification Events," *Evolution* 41 (1988): 1183.

¹¹ M. Denton, *Evolution: A Theory in Crisis* (Bethesda, MD: Adler and Adler, 1986), 191, 192.

¹² See J. A. Clack, *Gaining Ground: The Origin and Evolution of Tetrapods* (Bloomington, IN: Indiana University Press, 2002), 68–77.

¹³ E. B. Daeschler, N. H. Shubin, and F. A. Jenkins, "A Devonian Tetrapod-Like Fish and the Evolution of the Tetrapod Body Plan," *Nature* 44 (2006): 757–763.

¹⁴ G. Niedzwiedzki et al., "Tetrapod Trackways From the Early Middle Devonian Period of Poland," *Nature* 463 (2010): 43–48.

¹⁵ See, for example, C. de Muizon, "Walking With Whales," *Nature* 413 (2001): 259, 260.

177

Chapter 16

Is the Theory of Evolution Scientific?

Is the theory of evolution scientific? The search for an answer interfaces with other chapters in this book and likewise involves worldviews, data and its interpretation, as well as other issues. The easy answer is "Yes, it is scientific," but before we understand what that means, we need to ask what makes any theory scientific.

Science and religion

Science is a process of searching for answers.[1] An idea may be labeled scientific if it can be studied using the scientific method. If we have an idea and would like to know if it is a good one, several approaches can help us decide whether it is correct. First, we can use our own reasoning ability to decide whether we believe the idea to be true. We can also ask God to tell us whether it is true. This approach, asking God or looking for an answer in the Bible, is a religious approach. Finally, we can think of observations or experiments that may help determine whether the idea is correct. This approach is science. Let's compare these three approaches.

If we just think about it, how do we know our conclusion is correct? We need to compare our thoughts against some kind of standard. If we have no such standard, our thinking is just a wild guess. If we wonder how many teeth a horse has, will it be more helpful to think about how many teeth a horse should have or to open a horse's mouth and count them? We could ask God or search the Bible for the answer to the question about the number of horse's teeth. The problem is that the Bible was not given to us to answer questions such as this—questions that we can easily answer for ourselves and that have no spiritual significance. The Bible was given to answer other types of questions, which we will consider shortly. Regarding the question of how many teeth a horse has, isn't it more helpful to open a horse's mouth and count them? If we do so, we are using science to answer the question.

The scientific method may be described with the following sequence of events. A scientist has an idea, called a hypothesis, and then thinks of observations and experiments that will test the hypothesis. The observations are made, the experiments are conducted, and the results may indicate the hypothesis is false or may support it. Another possible outcome is that the answer will remain unclear, and different observations and experiments will have to be designed to better test the hypothesis. One thing we can be sure of—science will not provide us with absolute proof or disproof. We may think we have proof, but it is always possible that new evidence will change the picture. Only in TV commercials does science provide proof!

I sometimes tell my science students that half of what I am teaching is untrue. However, we'll have to wait for new scientific discoveries to show us which half is wrong! Some years ago the scientific evidence indicated there were ten species of chipmunks in California, but new evidence showed the existence of thirteen species. In molecular genetics, a concept once referred to as *the central dogma* was that each gene on our chromosomes directs the making of a single protein. However, new discoveries have shown the process to be significantly more complicated. The list of such changes in scientific understanding is endless. Science makes many significant discoveries, but in its continual progress, it keeps showing us that things we once were sure of are actually incorrect. We just didn't have enough evidence at the time to realize that our interpretation was not correct.

There are some ideas for which scientific study cannot offer us an answer due to their nature. They cannot be tested, no matter how much research is done. For example, when Jesus lived on earth, did He really perform miracles? Try to devise an experiment to test that idea, and you'll find it simply can't be done. Jesus' life on earth was long ago, and we were not there. Some of us are absolutely sure that He did actually perform miracles, but this belief cannot be proved with science. There is more to life and more to knowledge than just science. Science is an excellent way to discover many things, but it's important to acknowledge the limits of what questions science can answer for us.

Evolution

Now back to our question about the theory of evolution. To give an answer that is not superficial, we need to consider the meaning of the word *evolution*. One basic definition of biological evolution is change through time. Animals and plants change as their genetic system allows them to adapt to different environmental conditions. There are complexities in the process that we don't need to deal with here,[2] but the essential part of the definition is the change that occurs in populations of organisms as time passes. A simple example is the beaks of finches on the Galapagos Islands. The climate changed over a period of several years, resulting in changes in the finches' food supply. Individuals with beak sizes that didn't allow the food to fit well had less of chance of survival, and the average size of finch beaks changed to accommodate the available food. Then, as the climate shifted back to its previous condition, the available food also changed and the average finch beak size returned to what it was before the climate shifts.[3] This is an example of microevolution, change within a species, which generally occurs through mutations and natural selection.

Another example happens all the time in places like hospitals. For decades we have been using antibiotics to kill bacteria, but a few individual bacteria remain after the antibiotic kills off all the other bacteria. The result is strains of bacteria that are immune to our treatments, and thus very hard to control. This is also microevolution. Microevolution doesn't really make any new types of animals; it just allows species of animals or plants to adapt to changing environmental conditions.

The theory of evolution includes another concept—the evolution of all life forms, through long ages of time, from a common ancestor. This part of evolution says that toads, sparrows, worms, cabbage, palm trees, lobsters, and scientists are all the result of evolution; they evolved through time from a common, one-celled ancestor. We will simply refer to this as descent from a common ancestor.

Can either or both of these ideas about evolution be studied by the methods of science?[4] Yes, they definitely can. Many scientists conduct research on microevolution, observing how creatures change as the environment changes. They use observations and experiments to test hypotheses about these changes. They are studying processes that can be observed and documented. What about the larger changes through time—descent from common ancestors? Can this be studied with the methods of science? Yes, scientists use many types of evidence to develop and test hypotheses about evolution from common ancestors.

Both types of evolution are scientific in the sense that they can be studied with the methods of science. However, there is a difference between them. At least parts of the microevolution process can be observed, but descent of different types of animals from common ancestors in the distant past cannot be observed. Research on common descent does make use of scientific evidence, but it is much more dependent on assumptions in order to interpret that evidence. The most important assumption that is generally accepted by scientists claims there have never been any miracles, any supernatural acts, in all of history. In other words, everything in nature can be explained by the laws of nature that have been discovered. This is the assumption of naturalism, the worldview that doesn't accept the possibility of creation or intelligent design. Whenever this assumption is made, scientists will always interpret evidence according to the theory of common descent through evolution. The evidence can be interpreted in various ways, but in the naturalistic worldview, the only interpretations that will be accepted are those based on descent of all organisms from a common ancestor through evolution.

Many of us want to know more—not just whether the theory of evolution can be studied with science, but whether or not it is true. Sometimes the term *scientific* is used in a way that implies that if something is not scientific, it is not true. Since Jesus' miracles can't be tested by science, does that mean they are not true? That is not a reasonable conclusion. Science can't show that Jesus' miracles happened, neither can it show that they didn't occur. Science simply has nothing to say about it.

What does this tell us about evolution? Can the assumption of naturalism be tested by the methods of science? If it could, it would no longer be an assumption. The supposition that there were no supernatural acts involved in the origin of life forms (that is, no creation) is a belief about the past. It cannot be tested by observations or experiments. For this reason, the assumption is an arbitrary philosophical choice, not a choice that rests on science. There is considerable evidence that is claimed to support evolution over millions of years, but different worldviews can lead to different interpretations of the evidence. The difference is in the interpretations, and in the assumptions on which those interpretations depend. Science can provide evidence for us to think about but cannot show us *how* to understand that evidence.

We do experience some difficulty in explaining some of the evidence in biology and geology according to a biblical view of creation; however, there are also many types of evidence that are difficult to reconcile with the theory of millions of years of evolution. Since we were not there and don't have all the evidence, science does not have definitive answers to origins, and it is wise to seek God's answers to these questions.[5]

To illustrate this difference in worldviews and the resulting interpretations, consider this example: worms and scientists have the same biochemical processes occurring in the cells of their bodies. Naturalistic scientists think this indicates they evolved from the same common ancestor, but it could also mean that the same Creator designed both, using the same biochemical mechanism to maintain life in their cells. The difference between those two interpretations, evolution or creation, cannot be tested by the methods of science because they are based on assumptions about what happened in the past.

In study of microevolution we can often "open the horse's mouth and count the teeth." But when we ask if we evolved from bacteria and worms, we are asking a question about ancient history when no scientist was there to "open the horse's mouth." We can ask God for the answer, and in this case it is a spiritually significant question that the Bible does address. The only other option to answer the question is philosophical in nature—we can think about the limited evidence we have and decide, in our own heads, that the assumption of naturalism is correct. Is this a satisfying approach? Does God obey that assumption, or is He amazed at our naivety?

My last name is Brand. My father asked an expert in genealogical study to trace our ancestry, and he traced our history back to some prominent families in England. The problem was that the expert had made a false assumption—the supposition that the last name had been used in a consistent form through time. What he didn't know was that Grandfather Brandt, a German peasant farmer, named his first half dozen offspring "Brandt," but on the birth certificates of the last half dozen he named them "Brand." Arriving at a correct genealogical interpretation of origins depended on knowing that the history of the name had been changed by an intelligent choice. (I assume it was intelligent, but nobody knows why he did it; and yes, there were a dozen.) Our name had not been subject to the typical laws governing the descent of family names. So it is in science; if intelligent choice or creation was involved in the origin of groups of animals and plants, science will not recognize it if the scientists investigating this idea depend on a false assumption about origins.

Conclusion

Is the theory of evolution scientific? Yes, it is scientific in the sense that it can be studied by the methods of science. Does this mean that it is true? Does its status as a scientific theory make it a demonstrated fact? Many books written by scientists stoutly assert that evolution is a fact, as much so as gravity. However, those claims are not realistic if one possesses a proper understanding of the scientific method. Parts of evolution, especially microevolution, are well-documented and seem essentially true, although there may still be much to learn before we understand even that part correctly. This uncertainty is not unique to the study of evolution; in all of science the discovery of new phenomena keeps improving upon or correcting scientific ideas.

Other parts of evolution—for example, its claims about ancient history and the origin of life forms—are in a different category. Science can study these claims and devise hypotheses, but those hypotheses can never be rigorously tested by science. We were not there, and our interpretations of the ancient past are only as good as our assumptions. The claims are not scientific, if by "scientific" we mean they are demonstrated to be true; however, that is not really what the term *scientific* means.

I suggest that the level of confidence any one person has in the truth of evolutionary history (that is, common descent of all organisms) directly reflects the degree of confidence they have that science is the surest way of finding truth in any topic, and/or the confidence they have in the assumption of naturalism. Our confidence that God has spoken to us in His Word, the Bible, and has given a true history of life on earth is the basis of our Christian worldview. Thus, for many of us, the Word of God is a more reliable guide to understanding ancient history. God was there when life was created, and we were not. In the case of origins, He "counted the horse's teeth" and told us the answer. Unlike the question of the horse's teeth, the Bible does address the topic of origins because it is important for us to know where we came from, why we are here, and where we are going.

The question "Do I know Jesus?" may not seem very scientific, and to some may not be considered relevant to our decision about evolution. However, I submit that it is the most important question of all. Do we give more credence to contemporary scientific interpretations than to God's Word, or do we know Jesus well enough to have confidence in His communication to us through the Bible?

Leonard Brand received his BA in biology at La Sierra College, an MA in biology at Loma Linda University, and a PhD in evolutionary biology from Cornell University. He then joined the biology faculty at Loma Linda University in 1969 and has taught there since then. He is chairman of the Department of Earth and Biological Sciences, and professor of biology and paleontology. He studied geology as well as biology and has been active in research and has published numerous articles in biology and geology research journals, in addition to three books, many articles in church-sponsored journals, and numerous presentations on faith and science topics on several continents.

References

[1] L. Brand, *Faith, Reason and Earth History: A Paradigm of Earth and Biological Origins by Intelligent Design,* 2nd ed. (Berrien Springs, MI: Andrews University Press, 2009).

[2] Brand (2009); L. Brand, *Beginnings: Are Science and Scripture Partners in the Search for Origins?* (Nampa, ID: Pacific Press®, 2006).

[3] P. A. Grant, *Ecology and Evolution of Darwin's Finches* (Princeton, NJ: Princeton University Press, 1999).

[4] Brand (2006, 2009); D. Ratzsch, *Science and Its Limits: The Natural Sciences in Christian Perspective* (Downers Grove, IL: InterVarsity Press, 2000); J. P. Moreland, *Christianity and the Nature of Science* (Grand Rapids, MI: Baker Books, 1989).

[5] Brand (2006, 2009); S. C. Meyer, *Signature in the Cell: DNA and the Evidence for Intelligent Design* (New York: HarperCollins, 2009); A. A. Roth, *Origins: Linking Science and Scripture* (Hagerstown, MD: Review and Herald, 1998); A. A. Snelling, *Earth's Catastrophic Past: Geology, Creation & the Flood,* vols. 1 and 2 (Dallas, TX: Institute for Creation Research, 2009).

Chapter 17

Where Do Humans Come From?

The creationist understanding of Scripture, where humans are the product of a divine act of special creation, conflicts with the evolutionary hypothesis of descent with modification from ancestral primates. This chapter reviews and discusses the fossil evidence relating to human origins.

How do we decide what is a human?

A simple approach is to define humanity on the basis of anatomical characteristics. However, every living species shows variability of morphological traits. When compared with other extant primate species, modern humans' skeletal metrics appear to be rather homogeneous.[1] Certain fossils fall outside this limited modern spectrum of variability, and there is no clear consensus on the diagnostic criteria that should determine whether they should be considered humans or not. A practical approach is to place a given fossil in the *Homo* category when body mass and proportions, dental dimensions, and skeletal adaptations for bipedality show greater similarity to modern humans than to australopithecine fossils (a group of hominids whose remains were first recovered in Africa early in the last century). Other traits often considered relevant in defining humanity are brain dimensions, tool-making ability, and indications of social and symbolic behavior.

Did humans evolve from australopithecines?

In the evolutionary hypothesis, *Australopithecus* is considered the form from which *Homo* stemmed. Its remains are found in Pliocene deposits that lie beneath those containing *Homo* fossils. The anatomy of *Australopithecus* reveals traits that today can only be found in humans. However, many characteristics clearly distinguish *Australopithecus* from *Homo*. These include, among others: (1) a smaller body mass; (2) a small brain size (~400 to 550 cm^3 as opposed to ~1400 cm^3 of modern humans); (3) a greater length of forearm relative to upper arm; (4) a funnel-shaped chest; and (5) relatively long and curved fingers.[2]

Discoveries in recent decades have increased the range of variability observed in australopithecine fossils. As a result, a variety of species names have been applied to the remains. Further complications emerge from the discovery of *Ardipithecus ramidus* in layers beneath those containing *Australopithecus* remains. Despite its spatial and temporal proximity to *Australopithecus*, *Ardipithecus ramidus* is remarkably different.[3] On the other hand, layers above the stratigraphic range of *Australopithecus* yield remains assigned to *Homo* as well as fossils of hominids similar to *Australopithecus*, only with more robust skeletal features (genus *Paranthropus*). If both forms derived from *Australopithecus*, the discontinuity between *Homo* and *Australopithecus* becomes even more apparent when compared to the similarity between *Australopithecus* and *Paranthropus*.

In conclusion, the fossil evidence used to argue in favor of the evolutionary relationship between *Homo* and other extinct hominid forms is far from compelling and remains unresolved, particularly in the light of an as yet incomplete Pliocene hominid fossil record.

Does *Homo habilis* link australopithecines and humans?

Established in the1960s, *Homo habilis* is a species based mostly on fossil remains that have been discovered in eastern Africa. These fossils show such a great degree of morphological variation that many researchers believe the species actually contains two separate forms, one smaller sized and one larger. Cranial capacity estimates vary between 500 and 750 cm^3—slightly larger than the average of 400–550 cm^3 for australopithecines. Foot bone studies suggest that *H. habilis* was a terrestrial biped, but its arm bone proportions were apelike. Some authors have concluded that *H. habilis* is a derived form of australopithecine rather than part of the *Homo* genus.[4]

The "nonmodern looking" humans

Some fossils share enough similarities with anatomically modern humans (AMH) to be considered part of the genus *Homo*; however, they display traits distinctive enough to be described as different species. The following section discusses the main types of "nonmodern looking" human fossils.

Homo erectus. This species is based on discoveries made in Indonesia, China, Africa, and western Eurasia. Distinctive features of

H. erectus include (1) an elongated and low cranial vault; (2) robust brow ridges; (3) a sharp angle between the base and the posterior part of the cranium; and (4) an average absolute brain size (~1000 cm³) smaller than that of AMH. Postcranial[5] remains and well-preserved footprint trails indicate essentially modern body proportions and movement (locomotion). Estimated height and body mass for some *H. erectus* specimens is comparable to average AMH, but other specimens show very diminutive size.[6]

Among the enigmas surrounding the origin of *H. erectus* are its sudden appearance, its morphological discontinuity, and its co-occurrence with supposed ancestral forms. Another puzzle is that from the very beginning, *H. erectus* presents a wide geographic distribution— from Africa to Southeast Asia. This has led some to question the commonly accepted scenario of an African origin of *H. erectus* with subsequent dispersal to Asia. These researchers support the opposite view: origin in Asia and successive dispersal to Africa.[7]

Further, anthropologists disagree about the fate of *H. erectus*. Some argue that modern Asians preserve traits typical of *H. erectus*, suggesting regional continuity between AMH and *H. erectus* forms.[8] Others propose that Asian *H. erectus* was a long-lived peripheral side branch that eventually went extinct.[9]

Homo heidelbergensis. *H. erectus* fossils disappear from Africa and Europe towards the end of the lower Pleistocene. Here, they are succeeded by mid-Pleistocene fossils showing a marked increase in cranial capacity. These specimens have been grouped in the *H. heidelbergensis* species, seen as an African-European form derived from *H. erectus* and ancestral to both Neanderthals and AMH.[10]

Fossil remains found in the upper mid-Pleistocene of China are very similar to the classic African-European *H. heidelbergensis* specimens. Some authors suggest the Chinese material indicates a late migration to the Far East by *H. heidelbergensis.* However, supporters of the regional continuity view (where fossils from the same region that are apparently from different species show similarities) prefer to interpret the Chinese fossils to be evidence for local continuous gradation from *H. erectus* to AMH.[11]

Neanderthals *(Homo neanderthalensis).* Neanderthal fossils are found only in Europe and western Asia.[12] They show overall similarity to AMH but have a more robust skeletal structure and highly distinctive skull features.[13] Remains with the complete set of Neanderthal traits begin to occur in the upper Pleistocene, but Neanderthal-like characteristics are already apparent in mid-Pleistocene European hominid fossils.[14]

Neanderthals had body proportions similar to those of AMH living in extremely cold environments, for example, Eskimos. However, the idea that Neanderthal skeletal anatomy is a result of climate adaptation has recently been challenged. Interestingly, the Mediterranean region, with its mild climate, seems to have been their favorite residence.[15]

Neanderthals disappear from the fossil record in the uppermost Pleistocene. Some think their extinction was due to their replacement by new AMH migrants. Others propose that Neanderthals admixed at least in part with the expanding AMH group. Analysis of mitochondrial DNA (mtDNA) extracted from Neanderthal bones has revealed sequences that differ from the mtDNA of both modern and fossil AMH.[16] Nevertheless, these differences cannot completely rule out that Neanderthals contributed to the human genetic pool. In fact, a recent study of the Neanderthal genome seems to indicate that the DNA of present-day human populations carries segments derived from Neanderthals.[17]

The fossil record of anatomically modern humans

AMH are distinguished on the basis of a few traits, including, among others: (1) a skull with globular rather than elongated shape; (2) a face that does not project forward; (3) little development of brow ridges; (4) a well-defined chin; and (5) smaller dental dimensions.[18]

The earliest fossils showing this combination of traits come from East Africa. However, it's important to note that other contemporaneous specimens from the same localities do not look so modern.[19] It is only at a higher stratigraphic level (usually dated at around forty-five thousand years) that AMH become the dominant type of human fossil. At that point, they begin to be found from Europe to Australia to the Far East. The sudden expansion seems to correlate with dispersal from Western Asia. Soon after the expansion, the first striking examples of figurative arts (cave paintings and sculpted figurines) are recorded in Europe.

This pattern of appearance of modern morphological traits has led to the "Out of Africa" hypothesis, which posits that AMH evolved in East Africa first and later spread to the rest of the world. The mosaic of morphological characters apparent in most of the early AMH could be explained by the existence of some admixture with preexisting human populations (such as Neanderthals in Europe) instead of total replacement. An alternative model, the multiregional evolution theory, does not support the idea that AMH originated in Africa. Instead, it suggests that the emergence of anatomical modernity was a gradual process involving more than one population at a time. These groups would have been living in different regions but could have still exchanged genes, contributing to the overall gradual modification of our species.

Discussion

The significance of variability in morphological characters. Hominid species are defined on the assumption that morphological variability reflects genetic differences significant enough to preclude interbreeding. In other words, the species were so different from each other that they did not mix and produce offspring. However, some traits may vary for reasons other than genetics, for example, behavior and climate. Moreover, some skeletal differences that seem to imply biological discontinuity may instead be correlates of size or developmental stage, or may simply reflect a larger amount of variability than that observed in modern humans.[20]

Another complication with evolutionary reconstructions comes from the practice of assigning an order of appearance to morphological characters, defining some as "ancestral" or "primitive" and others as "derived." The distribution of these characteristics does not always follow the expected pattern, and mosaic combinations occur, where old fossils show "modern" traits or modern populations possess "archaic" traits.[21]

Notwithstanding the difficulties in interpreting variability in morphological characters, it cannot be denied that anatomical modernity appears only at the very top of the human fossil record.

Strengths and weaknesses of the evolutionary model. Previous sections of this chapter illustrate how current thought regarding human evolution is far from resolved. How to evaluate the current weight of evidence is obviously a subjective matter, but the writer's personal view is that the case for human evolution based on the study of fossils is not a compelling one. In particular, key transitions, such as the one from australopithecines to *Homo*, lack adequate detailed support to be demonstrated unequivocally. On the other hand, the evolutionary model's major strength lies in the ordered distribution of fossils, with australopithecines occurring below *Homo*, and AMH appearing only at the top of *Homo*'s stratigraphic range.[22]

Understanding the fossil evidence from a creationist perspective. The anatomical differences observed between australopithecines and *Homo* are interpreted by most creationists as representing two separate and nonrelated primate groups. The variability observed among different *Homo* species, however, is often interpreted as expression of high original diversity and microevolution within the human group.[23] According to this approach, *H. erectus, H. heidelbergensis, H. neanderthalensis,* and other "mosaic" forms would be true representatives of the human species that at some point developed distinctive sets of morphological traits as a result of genetic changes and ecological factors. This interpretation implies that the modern aspect of humans became fixed only relatively recently out of a greater range of morphological expressions. In fact, post-Flood microevolutionary modifications are routinely invoked for other species (like cats or canids) and should not be categorically ruled out for humans. Fixity of our species does not seem to be supported by scriptural evidence, and indeed, most creationists even propose that physiological changes occurred to our species as a consequence of sin or modified ecological conditions after the Flood.

Different human groups, such as *H. erectus* and *H. neanderthalensis,* could therefore represent post-Flood dispersals of populations that in some cases fixed certain anatomical traits because of their relative geographical isolation. The late appearance of AMH might be related to a more recent dispersal of a human group in which anatomically modern traits were predominant.[24] It is interesting to note that Scripture allows for such successive migrations (for example, the post-Flood dispersion, the post–Tower of Babel dispersion) and that the biblical and part of the fossil record converge in placing western Asia as the spreading center for these dispersals.

Ronny Nalin obtained his education at the University of Padova, Italy, where he graduated with a PhD in earth sciences. From 2007, he has worked as a research scientist at the Geoscience Research Institute, and is adjunct professor of geology at Loma Linda University, U.S.A. His research interests focus on sedimentology of nontropical carbonates, especially from the Mediterranean area, and sequence stratigraphy of shallow marine sedimentary deposits. He has published several papers on these subjects on international journals. His personal spiritual journey has gradually led him to value faith and science as sources of knowledge and understanding in life.

References

[1] M. M. Lahr, *The Evolution of Modern Human Cranial Diversity: A Study in Cranial Variation* (Cambridge: Cambridge Univ. Press, 1996).

[2] B. Asfaw et al., "*Australopithecus Garhi:* A New Species of Early Hominid From Ethiopia," *Science* 284 (1999): 629–635; B. Wood and M. Collard, "The Human Genus," *Science* 284 (1999): 65–71.

[3] T. White et al., "*Ardipithecus Ramidus* and the Paleobiology of Early Hominids," *Science* 326 (2009): 75–86.

[4] Wood and Collard (1999), see endnote 2.

[5] The word *postcranial* refers to skeletal elements other than the skull.

[6] D. Lordkipanidze et al., "Postcranial Evidence From Early *Homo* From Dmanisi, Georgia," *Nature* 449 (2007): 305–310; A. C. Walker and R. E. F. Leakey, *The Nariokotome* Homo Erectus *Skeleton* (Cambridge, MA: Harvard Univ. Press, 1993).

[7] R. Dennel and W. Roebroeks, "An Asian Perspective on Early Human Dispersal From Africa," *Nature* 438 (2005): 1099–1104.

[8] D. A. Elter, "The Fossil Evidence for Human Evolution in Asia," *Annual Review of Anthropology* 25 (1996): 275–301.

[9] C. B. Stringer, "Modern Human Origins: Progress and Prospects," *Philosophical Transactions of the Royal Society of London B* 357 (2002): 563–579.

[10] Stringer (2002), endnote 10.

[11] Elter (1996), endnote 9; Stringer (2002), endnote 10.

[12] Neanderthals may have ranged as far as southern Siberia.

[13] See E. Trinkaus, "Modern Human Versus Neandertal Evolutionary Distinctiveness," *Current Anthropology* 47, no. 4 (2006): 597–620, endnote 19.

[14] For example, the "Swanscombe skull." See C. B. Stringer and J. J. Hublin, "New Age Estimates for the Swanscombe Hominid, and Their Significance for Human Evolution," *Journal of Human Evolution* 37 (1999): 873–877. See also the skeletal remains discovered at Sima de los Huesos, Spain. J. L. Arsuaga et al., "The Sima de los Huesos Crania (Sierra de Atapuerca, Spain). A Comparative Study," *Journal of Human Evolution* 33 (1997): 219–281.

[15] P. Shipman, "Separating 'Us' from 'Them': Neanderthal and Modern Human Behavior," *Proceedings, National Academy of Sciences* (U.S.A.) 105, no. 38 (2008): 14241, 14242.

[16] J. P. Noonan et al., "Sequencing and Analysis of Neanderthal Genomic DNA," *Science* 314 (2006): 1113–1118.

[17] R. E. Green et al., "A Draft Sequence of the Neandertal Genome," *Science* 328 (2010): 710–722.

[18] E. Trinkaus, "Early Modern Humans," *Annual Review of Anthropology* 24 (2005): 207–230.

[19] M. H. Day, "Omo Human Skeletal Remains," *Nature* 222 (1969): 1135–1138.

[20] A. Rosas, "A Gradient of Size and Shape for the Atapuerca Sample and Middle Pleistocene Hominid Variability," *Journal of Human Evolution* 33 (1997): 319–331; T. White, "Early Hominids— Diversity or Distortion?" *Science* 299 (2003): 1994–1997.

[21] Trinkaus (2006), 597–620.

[22] The ordered distribution of biological remains is a major feature of the fossil record.

[23] M. L. Lubenow, *Bones of Contention* (Grand Rapids, MI: Baker Books, 2004).

[24] S. Hartwig-Scherer, "Apes or Ancestors?" in *Mere Creation*, W. A. Dembski, ed. (Downers Grove, IL: InterVarsity Press, 1998), 212–235.

Chapter 18

What Are the Moral Implications of Darwinism?

Every society or culture has a story explaining the origin of human beings. That story forms the foundation for the group's laws and morality.[1] Western civilization arose among people who believed the universe was the special creation of a loving God, who superintended His Creation within a framework of natural laws that we, in turn, could discover and use to improve our lives. If mankind is Creation's crown, then human life should be regarded as sacred.

In denying a Creator, Darwinism proposes a complete change in the definition and application of morality. Instead of "In the beginning God created the heavens and the earth," this naturalistic "origins myth"[2] begins with something like "In the beginning were the particles."[3] This alternative was first proposed by the ancient Greeks[4] but was brought to prominence in modern times by Charles Darwin. Thus, we will call it Darwinism in this chapter. This perspective has become entrenched among the intellectual elites in much of the world. Despite very real changes in law and morality that occur once the Darwinist worldview gains ascendance in a given society, little thought has been given to the consequences of the shift from a theistic to an atheistic moral foundation.

In this chapter we will look at several issues: (1) the tenets of Darwinism that impact morality; (2) the logical outgrowth of adopting those tenets as a basis for law and culture; and (3) examples showing the real-world consequences for each of us.

Darwinism and human nature

Darwinism proposes that life on earth is the result of an unguided process involving the random interactions of nonliving chemicals on the early earth. Once the first living cell formed and its genetic systems were in place, random changes in the DNA code gradually built new and different forms. After hundreds of millions of years, hominids emerged in Africa. These early "prehumans" gradually became modern human beings, via random DNA mutations selected by the environment over thousands of generations. As George Gaylord Simpson declared, "Man is the result of a purposeless and natural process that did not have him in mind."[5]

The most important claim of Darwinism is that the apparent design of living things, from the intricacies of our cellular machinery to the complex organs and tightly integrated organ systems of complete organisms, can be described as the result of a mindless, undirected, and completely natural process. No designer (and certainly no God), was necessary—everything about the living world, from the operations of our bodies and brains to the religious and moral lives that we live, is explained by reference to energy, matter, physical law, and time.[6]

Implications of Darwinism for morality

Instead of viewing humans as created in God's image, Darwinism sees them as simply an extension and elaboration of certain animals, distinctive only in features and abilities. Logically, if man is not essentially different, then he should not be treated as if he were; that is, under the Darwinian worldview laws that "privilege" human beings in comparison to other members of the animal kingdom are illogical. The animal rights movement, which coalesced with the publication of *Animal Liberation*,[7] is a clear result of this perspective. Peter Singer achieved fame (or perhaps notoriety) by seriously suggesting that we should act on Darwin's insights; that we should not always prefer human beings simply because they are human; and that in some cases certain animals have a stronger claim to life than certain humans.

Although Christians have long opposed cruelty to animals, they have not regarded animals as equal with humans, basing their views on texts such as Exodus 20:10, Proverbs 12:10, and Luke 12:6, 7. However, animal rights activists have moved well beyond the animal welfare efforts of the last century, and some assert that at times it is morally preferable to use human beings rather than chimpanzees for medical research. In the minds of these activists, our laws should stop favoring members of *Homo sapiens* over nonhuman species simply because they are humans, just as we attempt to stop the favoring of males over females, and of one race over another. A new and different set of criteria must be developed to determine what moral decisions should be made.

Created from animals?

Perhaps the most comprehensive attempt to work out how our society should be reordered according to a Darwinist reality was published by the late James Rachels, formerly a philosophy professor at the University of Alabama, Birmingham. His book *Created From Animals* attempts to work out Darwinism's moral implications. It is a relentlessly logical explanation of where naturalistic thinking leads, and if one grants Professor Rachels his premises, it becomes very difficult to argue with his major conclusion: that the proper view for a Darwinian is the ethic he calls "moral individualism."[8] Since man is not a special creation made in God's image but the result of an unguided, gradual process of evolution by natural selection over millennia, we are not different in kind from the nonhuman animal world. Thus, treating human beings, simply because they are human beings, differently than we do animals is "speciesist"—in other words, we express an unjustified bias that grants our species privileges that we refuse to other species.

The basic idea of "moral individualism," as proposed by Rachels, is that "how an individual may be treated is to be determined, not by considering his group memberships, but by considering his own particular characteristics."[9] Professor Rachels expected that this view would result in an improvement of the treatment of animals through widening the circle of moral obligation, which traditionally was applied to human beings. The broader circle would include animals, mammals showing evidence of higher brain function, for example, great apes, dolphins, and elephants. Of course, if higher brain function is to be the measure of one's moral status, then humans judged to lack the requisite brain function can be treated as if they were "lower" animals, which also lack such function. This logical yardstick legitimates the abortion of unborn humans, infanticide of very young children, euthanasia of the elderly and disabled, the creation of human embryos for destructive experimentation, and many other activities we have traditionally categorized as unacceptable and thus, criminal.

Rachels is careful to reassure his readers that "human life can still be valued, and we can still justify moral and legal rules to protect it. We will, however, have to acknowledge that these rules grow out of our own valuings, rather than descending to us from some higher authority. If that is a loss, it may be a loss that humans after Darwin must live with."[10] Or die with, of course, since the ethic that Rachels espouses imperils many of our fellow human beings, who have long been protected by our espousal of the sacredness of human life. If society deems humans no more special than any other species, the burden of those disabled and thus "useless" and/or expensive, does not have to be borne. They can be mercifully done away with without raising any moral qualms.

Some will say this extreme outcome merely represents the cogitations of an academic philosopher, with no real world application. Those tempted by the comfort of such thoughts would do well to read the current literature in bioethics. Even some Christian bioethicists have become "converts" to this Darwinist view. James Walters, in "Is Koko a Person?"[11] argues that "A person's unique moral claim to life depends primarily on his or her higher mental capacities. The individual being who will never possess—or is forever beyond possession of—neo-cortical functioning does not have a special moral claim to life." This Christian professor expresses agreement with Peter Singer that handicapped babies, disabled adults, and others may be killed under some circumstances. Among bioethicists, this position isn't shocking, but it is certainly a long way from the traditional Christian concept of the sacredness of human life.

Application of Darwinism to moral issues

So, what are the practical moral implications of Darwinism? Rather than speculate, we can look for evidence of how human beings are being treated in nations that have moved from a commitment to "the Laws of Nature and of Nature's God"[12] to an embrace of the Darwinian view of the origin of life and of mankind. Perhaps the easiest way to access trustworthy information, both about what is actually occurring and about what is being discussed, is to search the Internet using the term "Darwinian bioethics." Recent items included the following:[13]

- The Scottish Parliament's bill to allow active euthanasia by nonmedical people with no limitations on health status, age, or method of dealing death.
- Efforts by Compassion and Choices, an assisted suicide advocacy group, to eliminate the "conscience exception" to laws legalizing abortion, euthanasia, and other lethal "medical care," meaning that those who are unable to conscientiously kill a patient who wishes to die would be forced to violate their conscience or quit medical practice.
- The refusal to provide a new and highly effective ("life-changing") drug to British sufferers from rheumatoid arthritis by NICE, the UK's National Institute for Health and Clinical Excellence (it appears that nobody in the British government has read C. S. Lewis' *That Hideous Strength*[14]).

Examples such as these starkly illustrate the trajectory of the course taken when biblical principles are abandoned in favor of relativistic concepts that judge some human lives as valuable and therefore legally protected, but others less valuable and thus not protected. This is the logical entailment of a Darwinist view. William Provine, Cornell University professor in Biological Sciences, provides perhaps the most straightforward declaration about what Darwinism entails in regards to faith: "[R]eligion is compatible with modern evolutionary biology (and indeed all of modern science) *if the religion is effectively indistinguishable from atheism.*"[15]

The news is not unremittingly bad. One bright spot is "Team Hoyt," a story published in *Sports Illustrated* (no longer found on their Web site) but posted on YouTube.[16] Rick Hoyt was born severely disabled by cerebral palsy, and his parents were urged to "put him in an institution" because he would never walk, talk, or be anything but a vegetable. The family took him home and treated him like their other two boys. Over the years, Rick learned to communicate with the help of a computer, attended school, graduated from college, saved his father's life, and became a potent symbol of the value of every human being, regardless of "usefulness" or (dis)abilities. However, this type of story is considerably harder to find than the other kind. The trajectory of modern culture is illuminated by the outcry against former Alaska governor Sarah Palin's decision to give birth to her child after learning he had Down's syndrome.

Conclusion

We no longer need to guess where we will end up if we decide to continue "progressing" away from our theistic roots. Several countries in Europe are further along the path than many—most notably Switzerland, with its "euthanasia tourism,"[17] and the Netherlands, with its doctors euthanizing patients of all ages.[18] Those who wonder about what is really happening in specific cases and countries should seek out information on their own rather than trust popular media for objective reporting.

It is a logical certainty that, in the absence of a standard outside ourselves and without a renewed acceptance of the concept of "human exceptionalism," what will rule is our human nature—whether it is the result of our sinful condition or of millions of years of natural selection. Humans are naturally selfish—we are most interested in our own well-being and that of our relatives. If we design laws according to our inclinations, we will see to it that our own group is taken care of—the others not so much. In fact, when we perceive that our own well-being may be advanced by damaging someone else, we are likely to do the other person damage. This can be seen in the high incidence of abortion,[19] and in the ethnic and religious violence experienced in such places as Rwanda, Bosnia, Sudan, and on and on.

The Christian standard of morality requires all to "love your neighbor as yourself."[20] Despite constant failures in meeting this moral obligation, it has nevertheless encouraged protection of the poor, weak, and disabled much better than any system man has devised. When we adopt Darwinism as our "origins myth," we abandon this transcendent standard. Without it, morality devolves to some form of "might makes right"— those with more power rule and variously oppress those with less.[21] The twentieth century has provided us with at least three major cautionary examples in Soviet Russia, Nazi Germany, and Mao's China. The twenty-first continues the lesson we are so slow to absorb. We must pay closer attention and learn.

Earl M. J. Aagaard completed his BA degree at Pacific Union College (PUC), and served with his wife, Gail, as a student missionary at Colegio Adventista de Bolivia. He obtained a MA degree at PUC, and did further graduate work at Colorado State University. Following research in the Andes of Venezuela, he was awarded a PhD degree. After four years of secondary school teaching, he began twenty-two years in the PUC Biology Department, followed by five years at Southern Adventist University, from which he retired in 2009. He continues to write and lecture, as well as to participate in seminars on faith and science around the world.

References

[1] *Morality* refers to standards of conduct that distinguish right from wrong.

[2] *Origins myth* is a term referring to any story of origins that involves prehistoric supernatural activity. A "myth" can be true or false, but it cannot be verified empirically.

[3] http://www.gracevalley.org/sermon_trans/Special_Speakers/In_Beginning_Particles.html. "In the Beginning Were the Particles" by Dr. Phillip E. Johnson, edited transcript from a lecture sponsored by Grace Valley Christian Center, Sunday, March 5, 2000 (10 A.M.). "In the beginning were the particles. And the particles somehow became complex living stuff. And the stuff imagined God, but then discovered evolution."

[4] For example, see Lucretius, *On the Nature of Things.*

[5] G. G. Simpson, "Epilogue and Summary," in *The Meaning of Evolution* (New Haven, CT: Yale University Press, 1967), 345.

[6] R. Dawkins, *The Blind Watchmaker* (London: Penguin Books, Ltd., 1986).

[7] P. Singer, *Animal Liberation,* reissue ed. (New York: Harper Perennial Modern Classics, 2009).

[8] J. Rachels, *Created From Animals: The Moral Implications of Darwinism* (New York: Oxford University Press, 1990), 173.

[9] Ibid., 173.

[10] Ibid., 205.

[11] http://dialogue.adventist.org/articles/09_2_walters_e.htm.

[12] Wording from the American Declaration of Independence.

[13] View the archives at http://www.firstthings.com/blogs/secondhandsmoke.

[14] C. S. Lewis, *That Hideous Strength: A Modern Fairy-Tale for Grown-Ups,* 6th ed. (New York: Macmillan, 1965). The book describes a particularly awful group dealing out death. Ironically, the group is known by the acronym "NICE."

[15] W. B. Provine, review of *Trial and Error: The American Controversy over Creation and Evolution*, by Edward J. Larson, *Academe* 73 (January/February 1984): 51, 52; emphasis added.

[16] http://www.youtube.com/watch?v=ecwcq7FwHeY.

[17] http://www.health-insurance.org/assisted-suicide-travel.

[18] http://alexschadenberg.blogspot.com/2010/01/euthanasia-in-netherlands-continues-to.html.

[19] http://newsbusters.org/blogs/kyle-drennen/2008/09/18/msnbc-wapo-s-quinn-declares-90 -parents-abort-downs-syndrome-babies; www.blogher.com/down-syndrome-abortion-controversy.

[20] Leviticus 19:18; Matthew 19:19.

[21] http://www.answers.com/topic/might-makes-right.

Chapter 19

Can a Christian Be a Good Scientist?

Studying science can be one of life's most exciting and rewarding experiences. However, Christians studying science can sometimes be challenged by teachers and fellow students claiming that only people who are uneducated or ignorant of the discoveries in biology, geology, archaeology, and astronomy could still believe the Bible account is true. Let me reassure you that I have met and talked with many outstanding scientists who not only believe in the miracles of the Bible but also testify that the truths in God's Word have helped them be successful in their personal lives and in their scientific careers.[1] In fact it was Christian scientists who helped me to come to know Jesus as my Savior. Let me share my experience.

I began my career as a trainee physicist at the BHP Central Research Laboratories in Australia. (Now the world's largest mining company, in the 1960s BHP was already the largest steelmaker in the southern hemisphere.) I was appointed assistant to a recently arrived scientist who had been a university academic gold medalist and had just completed postdoctoral studies at Imperial College, London. He was a meticulous record-keeper. Every page in his log books was pre-stamped with a number, all results had to be recorded, all equipment needed to be kept in full calibration with reference standards regularly checked against primary standards. From him I learned the techniques of first-class research; he also talked to me about Jesus.

At the time, I was a nominal Christian who ticked the Methodist box on forms. Because my supervisor was a Christian concerned for my salvation, he urged me to read the book *Mere Christianity* by C. S. Lewis, which I did. This scientist's lifestyle was a sharp contrast to that of most others in our section, who had also been educated at top-flight institutions like Cambridge University and the Massachusetts Institute of Technology. They were usually either heavy smokers or drinkers. In my early teens, I had made my own decision to never smoke or drink. As I observed the apparent emptiness of these scientists' lives, who boasted of their drinking, and saw the contrast with the positiveness of my Christian mentor, I began to seriously ask questions such as, "Is there really a personal God?" and "How can I find out about God?"

Midway though my studies I changed from specialization in physics and mathematics to chemistry, and for my honors year I chose a project that would be supervised by the head of the university's Chemistry Department. As I worked for this professor, author of internationally published textbooks, I learned that he, too, was a Christian. Whenever I went to his office, I was greeted with a beaming smile and a hearty, "Come in John! What can I do for you?" This was usually followed up by some humorous comment such as, "Have you found a girlfriend yet?" He was never too busy to see me and always enthusiastically supported my research ideas while making guiding suggestions that I "might like to consider." This professor, who was known for his positive nature and interest in people, gave me such encouragement that I achieved top of my honors class and was awarded a prestigious academic prize.

Just after finishing my university degree, I decided to begin attending church. I chose to go to a nearby Seventh-day Adventist church because when my father had died some nine years earlier, a Seventh-day Adventist dentist had shown our family much kindness. Since this dentist knew I was studying science, he had given me a very expensive slide rule. (These were used in the days before pocket calculators.) I had looked up Sabbath in an encyclopedia and read that the biblical Sabbath was Saturday, so I knew that was the right day to go to church to worship God. I applied for a postgraduate research scholarship, and I remember my first prayer asked God to help me get it. A couple of months later, I received a positive answer to that prayer when I was awarded the Tioxide Research Fellowship—the highest-paying chemistry research scholarship then offered in Australia. I continued attending church on the Sabbath, and just over eighteen months later I accepted Jesus as my Savior and was baptized.

As I look back on those experiences of forty years ago, I praise God for His leading in my life. Not only have I personally experienced many positive answers to prayer and enjoyed excellent health from following biblical health principles, I've also learned about the archaeological evidence supporting the historical accuracy of the Bible[2] and have researched the evidence for the fulfilment of Bible prophecy.[3] I've also learned that many of the scientists who laid the foundations of modern science were Bible-believing Christians. These pioneering figures include

Isaac Newton, Robert Boyle, Johannes Kepler, Carl Linnaeus, Michael Faraday, Samuel Morse, Charles Babbage, Matthew Maury, James Joule, Louis Pasteur, George Mendel, Lord Kelvin, Joseph Lister, James Clerk Maxwell, and John Ambrose Fleming.[4] For example, Maury, a pioneering oceanographer, believed that the Bible could be used as a guide to understanding nature. After reading Psalm 8:8, which talks about the paths of the seas, he looked for these paths and discovered the ocean currents and much more.[5]

Leading philosophers such as Lynn White, who taught at Princeton, Stanford, and UCLA, recognize that it was Western Europe's Christian worldview dominating in the Middle Ages that provided the environment for science to flourish there, and not in other parts of the world where non-Christian cultures dominated.[6] Science could not make significant progress in these cultures because of the perceived risk of offending local gods or because the culture's focus was on discovering signs and purpose in nature. Within the Christian worldview, British scientist and philosopher Francis Bacon successfully proposed that scientists should work together to discover how nature worked, and thus improve the condition of humans. Following on from Bacon, French mathematician Rene Descartes believed that God had created mathematical order in the universe. He proposed that by studying small parts of nature in detail and summing the parts mathematically, the laws governing the universe could be discovered. Thus, the concept of reductionism was conceived. When the devout Christian and Bible scholar Isaac Newton discovered calculus, it opened the way for him to explain many of the laws of physics that we know today (for example, the laws of motion and the law of gravity). Thus, scientists who believed in God the Creator and the truths of the

Bible laid the foundations of modern science, which enabled subsequent generations of scientists to develop the technologies we enjoy today.[7]

As I think about the knowledge I have gained over the years, it makes me realize that it is those who have not read and learned the truths of the Bible who are in reality the ignorant ones. The characteristics of a good scientist, such as integrity, attention to detail, humility, willingness to recognize mistakes, inquisitiveness, the desire to search for and discover the truth, and caring for others and for the environment, are all aligned with, if not directly based upon, the biblical Christian worldview.

One aspect of science research that continues to challenge me, however, is the widespread acceptance of the theory of evolution as an explanation of how life came to be, although there is still no experimental evidence to support this theory. Biophysicist Lee Spetner, who taught information theory at Johns Hopkins University for many years, points out that there is no evidence of purposeful genetic information arising by chance mutations, and on the basis of probability theory, it is impossible.[8] Also, there is still no known mechanism that can explain how a living cell could arise from nonliving molecules.[9] In his latest book, Oxford University professor and atheist Richard Dawkins gives a single example that he claims is evidence of new purposeful genetic information arising by chance. This example relates to the work of Richard Lenski and his team of researchers at the Department of Microbiology and Molecular Genetics at Michigan State University.[10] However, Lenski and his colleagues are not sure of the mechanism that produced the change in genetic information, and both possible mechanisms proposed by the researchers involve preexisting genetic information.[11] In other words, the world's foremost advocate of evolution—Richard Dawkins—has not provided a single proven example of experimental evidence for the type of evolution that would be needed to produce the first eye, the first jointed legs, the first feathers, and the vast amount of new genetic information associated with all the different types of living things that exist. Leading educators admit there is still no known mechanism that explains how new purposeful genetic information can form. This remains a major research focus in biology. As one well-regarded educational Web site puts it, "Biologists are not arguing about these conclusions [that many biologists believe life on earth has evolved]. But they are trying to figure out how evolution happens—and that's not an easy job."[12]

Over the years, I have met many leading scientists who have realized that the scientific evidence we have available to us today strongly supports the Bible's account of how we came to be here.[13] I recently learned that former Cornell University geneticist John Sanford, inventor of the gene gun used in genetic engineering, has become a young-earth six-day creationist on the basis of scientific evidence showing that human DNA is deteriorating at an alarming rate, and thus cannot be millions of years old.[14]

Science is the study of God's creation. It involves observing nature and carrying out experiments that give us insights into how we can be the best stewards of His handiwork. Being a Christian and reading God's Word—the Bible—gives us added insights from the Creator Himself. The apostle Paul reminds us that we are God's workmanship, created in Christ Jesus to do the good works which God himself prepares for us to do (Ephesians 2:10). So, can a Christian be a good scientist? I will let you be the judge of that.

John F. Ashton holds a BSc with honors in chemistry and a PhD in epistemology from the University of Newcastle, Australia, and a MSc in chemistry from the University of Tasmania. He was elected a Fellow of the Royal Australian Chemical Institute in 1992 and has held senior positions in tertiary education and industrial research for more than thirty years. Currently he is the strategic research manager for the Sanitarium Health Food Company and also serves as adjunct associate professor of biomedical sciences at Victoria University, Australia. He has co-authored more than one hundred science related articles and research papers as well as a dozen books.

References

[1] J. F. Ashton, ed., *On the Seventh Day: 40 Scientists and Academics Explain Why They Believe in God* (Green Forest, AK: Master Books, 2003).

[2] J. Ashton and D. Down, *Unwrapping the Pharaohs: How Egyptian Archeology Confirms the Biblical Timeline* (Green Forest, AK: Master Books, 2007).

[3] J. F. Ashton, with foreword by B. McCusker, *The Seventh Millennium, the Evidence We Can Know the Future* (Sydney and London: New Holland, 1998).

[4] A. Lamont, *21 Great Scientists Who Believed the Bible* (Acacia Ridge, Qld: Creation Science Foundation, 1995).

[5] Ibid., 121–131.

[6] L. White, "The Historical Roots of Our Ecologic Crisis," *Science* 155 (March 10, 1967): 1203–1206.

[7] J. H. Randall, *The Making of the Modern Mind* (Boston: Houghton Mifflin Co., 1940).

[8] L. M. Spetner, *Not by Chance* (New York: Judaica Press, Inc., 1997), 85–160.

[9] A. Ricardo and J. W. Szostak, "Origin of Life on Earth," *Scientific American* 301 (September 2009): 38–45.

[10] R. Dawkins, *The Greatest Show on Earth: The Evidence for Evolution* (London: Bantam Press, 2009), 131.

[11] Z. D. Blount, C. Z. Borland, and R. E. Lenski, "Historical Contingency and the Evolution of a Key Innovation in an Experimental Population of *Escherichia Coli,*" *Proceedings of the National Academy of Sciences* 105, no. 23 (2008): 7899–7906.

[12] Evolution 101, "The Big Issues," http://evolution.berkeley.edu/evosite/evo101/VIIBigissues.shtml.

[13] J. Ashton, ed., *In Six Days: Why Fifty Scientists Choose to Believe in Creation* (Green Forest, AK: Master Books, 2007), http://creationontheweb.com/content/view/3323/ or http://www.creationontheweb.com/isd.

[14] http://creation.com/john-sanford. See also J. C. Sanford, *Genetic Entropy & the Mystery of the Genome* (Livonia, NY: Feed My Sheep Foundation, Inc., 2008).

Chapter 20

How Can I Live Without Having All the Answers?

The secret things belong to the LORD our God, but the things that are revealed belong to us and to our children forever, that we may do all the words of this law (Deuteronomy 29:29, ESV).

If we had perfect knowledge, our science and our theology would never be in conflict, because the same God who reveals Himself through Scripture has also revealed Himself through His creation, and God is not in conflict with Himself. Thus, when we see conflict between our best theology and our best science, we should recognize this merely indicates our lack of complete understanding. As one well-known Christian geologist states,

Because Scripture and the created universe are both God-given, they cannot be in conflict. They form one comprehensive, unified, coherent whole that is an expression of the character and will of our Creator and Redeemer, who is the author of both. Nature

and Scripture form a unity, because God himself is One. . . . The
Bible and nature sometimes seem to be unrelated to one another,
in competition with one another or even in conflict with one
another. Such disjunctions, however, lie not between the Bible
and the created order, but rather between human understanding
of the Bible and human understanding of nature. It is human
interpretations of God-given data that lead into discrepancy,
conflict and disagreement.[1]

When Christ returns to earth, we hope to gain greater understanding
and have some, though perhaps not all, of our questions answered. Until
then, how should we live with unanswered questions? Following are four
responses that I have found to be helpful.

1. Recognize that every discipline has its own unanswered questions.
In theology, Christians struggled for centuries to understand exactly
who Jesus is. It was clear from His life that Jesus was a human being
who experienced hunger and felt pain, like all humans. It was also clear
that Jesus was divine and accepted the worship of those He healed. How
could Jesus be both human and divine at the same time? It is a great
mystery. Although the Council of Nicea defined this mystery for the
early Christian church, stating that Jesus was both fully human and fully
divine, this did not explain how one person could be both divine and
human simultaneously.

Science also has its unanswered questions. For example, what is
light? For centuries, physicists struggled to understand its character.
Some experiments indicated that light consists of discrete particles, while

other experiments showed that light is spread out in waves. It wasn't until the development of quantum mechanics in the twentieth century that scientists understood light to be a quantum mechanical "wave-packet" that can exhibit wavelike or particlelike features depending upon the experiment that is selected. However, this only defines the mystery. It does not completely answer the question, because it is not clear exactly what quantum mechanics tells us about the nature of reality.

Most scientists and engineers are willing to accept the results of quantum mechanics without thinking too much about the philosophical questions of what light really is. Quantum mechanics explains the results of our experiments extremely well and has been successfully used to develop many important technological devices, such as the laser; the transistor; magnetic resonance imaging (MRI); and perhaps in the future, high-speed quantum computers. However, this still leaves unanswered the question of what light really is prior to being measured in an experiment. The answer is unimportant for the development of technology. For this reason, the standard interpretation of quantum mechanics has been characterized as the "shut up and calculate" interpretation, meaning, "don't worry about the philosophical ramifications of quantum mechanics—just use it."

Both theology and science have unanswered (and perhaps unanswerable) questions. But these are mysteries that are worth struggling with and trying to understand, because they point to some of the most important, fundamental truths about God and reality. Given that each discipline has unanswered questions at its core, we should not be surprised to find that attempts to reconcile science and theology lead to additional unanswered questions. This does not mean that science and theology are at war or that one side must win and the other lose. Rather, this provides yet another indication that God and reality are greater than we can comprehend. We need to recognize that these "conflicts" may point to important underlying truths. Resolution may not come easily, and these conflicts may not be completely resolvable in this life, but it is worth the attempt to better understand both God and His creation.

2. Investigate the ramifications for each discipline of accepting the "truths" of the other discipline. It is important to ask what would be the ramifications to our theology if we were to accept certain current scientific theories. Theologians after the time of Galileo found no violation of fundamental theological principles in accepting that the Earth orbits the Sun, rather than the Sun orbiting the Earth. Biblical statements that appeared to be in conflict with a moving Earth (for example, Joshua's command that the Sun stand still) were reinterpreted without damaging either of the important points being made in the text or the underlying theology. In cases like this, a clear understanding of Scripture can resolve conflicts. In other cases, the prevailing scientific theory may be found to be incompatible with Scripture. However, in either case, the examination process helps reaffirm the most important theological points. This does not mean that theologians must accept all scientific theories, nor that science trumps theology. But in some cases, conflict can be avoided by recognizing that an apparent conflict need not exist.

Likewise, it is important for Christians who are scientists to investigate the ramifications of Christian beliefs for science. Some of the best science has been carried out by individuals willing to think outside the box and investigate nonconventional hypotheses and theories. The greatest accomplishment of nineteenth century physics was James Clerk Maxwell's development of electromagnetic field theory. Maxwell, a devout Christian, credited his understanding of the dynamic relationship of the triune God as an "analogical truth" that helped him to develop his dynamic electromagnetic field theory. "It was not that Clerk Maxwell imported theological conceptions as such into his science, but that it was the slant of his deeply Christian mind informed by faith that exercised a guiding role in the choice and formation of his leading scientific concepts."[2]

3. *Keep the discussion going.* In both theology and science, some of the most important truths arise out of conflict and contradiction. The proponents of Christ's humanity and the proponents of Christ's divinity both had to be heard. We would never have developed a complete picture of the nature of Christ if one side had been allowed to defeat and silence the other. Likewise, we would never have developed quantum mechanics if the scientists who believed that light was made up of discrete particles had been allowed to defeat and silence the scientists who believed that light was made up of waves, or vice versa. Even though in some cases we may not see how our understanding of science and our understanding of theology relate to each other, we cannot afford to silence either voice.

Albert Einstein recognized the need for science and theology to talk with each other in his expression, "Science without religion is lame; religion without science is blind."[3] That is, science must ultimately look outside itself to religion for a sense of meaning, and religion is ultimately about all of reality—not just the spiritual—and thus should not ignore the physical world. This relationship has been embraced by the physicist and theologian John Polkinghorne:

People who are seeking to serve the God of truth should welcome all truth from whatever source it may come, without fear or reserve. Included in this open embrace must certainly be the truths of science. In the case of the scientists, the same insight implies that if they want to pursue the search for understanding through and through—a quest that it is most natural for them to embark upon—they will have to be prepared to go beyond the limits of science itself in the search for the widest and deepest context of intelligibility. I think that this further quest, if openly pursued, will take the enquirer in the direction of religious belief.[4]

4. Recognize what is most important. Although we would like all of our questions answered, Jesus made it clear that He came to heal and to save, and that this was more important than answering questions. When His disciples met a man blind from birth, they asked why he was born blind, whether it was because of his own sin, or his parents' sin.[5] Jesus' response was that the man's blindness was not due to either cause. But He did not address the underlying assumption that adversities such as this man's blindness were a judgment from God because of sin. Rather, He simply stated that God's glory would be manifested through the man's blindness, and proceeded to heal the man. Solving the problem was far more important to Jesus than providing an explanation. As the theologian Thomas Tracy states,

The good news proclaimed in the New Testament is that God has acted to liberate and redeem, not that God has offered us a satisfactory accounting of why things are as they are. . . . We long for both liberation and comprehension, though neither is within our own power, and it is no surprise that the promise of God's unfailing love is a matter of more urgent concern than the prospect of a fuller explanation.[6]

As the gospel writers proceed to recount the sufferings and death of Jesus, no explanation is given for the existence of sin, suffering, and death—only that through Jesus' suffering and death, we can be saved. Ellen White wrote,

It is impossible to explain the origin of sin so as to give a reason for its existence. . . . Sin is an intruder, for whose presence no reason can be given. It is mysterious, unaccountable; to excuse it, is to defend it. Could excuse for it be found, or cause be shown for its existence, it would cease to be sin.[7]

Thus, although we would like to understand why the world is as it is, ultimately the gospel message is that the world needs redemption, and that a better world awaits us. Salvation is more important than explanation.

Conclusion

Frank Hasel has made the point that, "In science as well as in theology, humility is one of the rarest, yet most important, characteristics and presuppositions of those engaged in the study of both."[8] Science provides powerful tools to understand the intricate details of God's creation. However, as scientists push the edges of their disciplines to search for a more complete picture of the universe, they come to recognize that their explanations reveal an underlying reality that is still inexplicable. Thus, the true scientist is constrained by his discipline to be humble.

The theologian is similarly constrained. The Bible provides a reliable and trustworthy account of how God has interacted with people throughout history. It provides all that is needful for salvation. However, not all questions about God's nature are answered. There's always something more for the theologian to learn about God.

> "For my thoughts are not your thoughts, neither are your ways my ways, declares the LORD. For as the heavens are higher than the earth, so are my ways higher than your ways and my thoughts than your thoughts" (Isaiah 55:8, 9, ESV).

The theologian's striving for a complete picture of the transcendent God likewise requires humility.

Both the scientist and theologian "see through a glass, darkly." We see enough to gain certain knowledge regarding what God has revealed about Himself and His creation. However, the picture is still but a shadow of the reality. We look forward to the time when we will see clearly a more complete picture and join our disciplinary perspectives, for to learn about God's creation is also to learn about God.

> For now we see through a glass, darkly; but then face to face: now I know in part; but then shall I know even as also I am known (1 Corinthians 13:12, KJV).

Gary W. Burdick *is a physics and mathematics graduate of Southern Adventist University and received his PhD in physics from the University of Texas at Austin. He held postdoctoral positions in France, Hong Kong, and Virginia before joining the faculty at La Sierra University. He moved to Andrews University in 1999, where he is currently professor of physics and associate dean for research. In his research area of optical spectroscopy, dealing with electronic (optical) transitions of lanthanide elements in solid-state media, he has established international collaborations with various research labs. He has more than forty refereed scientific publications and many international conference presentations on his work.*

References

[1] Davis A. Young and Ralph F. Stearley, *The Bible, Rocks, and Time* (Downers Grove, IL: InterVarsity Press, 2008), 483, 484.

[2] Thomas F. Torrance, *Theological and Natural Science* (Eugene, OR: Wipf and Stock, 2002), 15.

[3] Albert Einstein, "Science and Religion," in *Ideas and Opinions,* 3rd ed. (New York: Three Rivers Press, 1995), 46.

[4] John Polkinghorne, *Quantum Physics and Theology* (New Haven, CT: Yale University Press, 2007), 109, 110.

[5] See John 9.

[6] Thomas F. Tracy, *Lawfulness of Nature, in Physics and Cosmology: Scientific Perspectives on the Problem of Natural Evil,* vol. 1 (n.p.: Vatican Observatory Publications, 2007), 155.

[7] Ellen G. White, *The Great Controversy* (Nampa, ID: Pacific Press®, 1950), 492, 493.

[8] Frank M. Hasel, "How to Deal With Open Questions: Facing the Challenges Between Faith and Science," *Ministry* 79, no. 7 (July 2007): 21–23.